Praise for the *Roots of Contemporary Issues Series*

Everything around us—policy, population, culture, economy, environment—is a product of the actions and activities of people in the past. How can we hope to address the challenges we face and resolve contentious issues—like inequality, health, immigration, and climate change—without understanding where they come from? The volumes in the Roots of Contemporary Issues series are the tested products of years of classroom teaching and research. They address controversial issues with impartiality but not detachment, combining historical context and human agency to create accounts that are meaningful and usable for any student confronting the complex world in which they will live.

—TREVOR T. GETZ, *San Francisco State University*

This is a truly innovative series that promises to revolutionize how world history is taught, freeing students and faculty alike from the "tyranny of coverage" often embedded within civilizational paradigms, and facilitating sustained reflection on the roots of the most pressing issues in our contemporary world. Students' understanding of the importance of history and their interest in our discipline is sure to be heightened by these volumes that deeply contextualize and historicize current global problems.

—NICOLA FOOTE, *Arizona State University*

ROOTS OF CONTEMPORARY ISSUES

HEAVY TRAFFIC

ROOTS OF CONTEMPORARY ISSUES

Series Editors

Jesse Spohnholz and Clif Stratton

The **Roots of Contemporary Issues** Series is built on the premise that students will be better at facing current and future challenges, no matter their major or career path, if they are capable of addressing controversial issues in mature, reasoned ways using evidence, critical thinking, and clear written and oral communication skills. To help students achieve these goals, each title in the Series argues that we need both an understanding of the ways in which humans have been interconnected with places around the world for decades and even centuries.

<u>Published</u>

Ruptured Lives: Refugee Crises in Historical Perspective
Jesse Spohnholz, Washington State University

Power Politics: Carbon Energy in Historical Perspective
Clif Stratton, Washington State University

Chronic Disparities: Public Health in Historical Perspective
Sean Wempe, California State University, Bakersfield

Heavy Traffic: The Global Drug Trade in Historical Perspective
Ken Faunce, Washington State University

<u>Forthcoming</u>

Gender Rules: Gender and Empire in Historical Perspective
Karen Phoenix, Washington State University

Heavy Traffic

The Global Drug Trade in Historical Perspective

Roots of Contemporary Issues

Ken Faunce

Washington State University

New York   Oxford
OXFORD UNIVERSITY PRESS

Oxford University Press is a department of the University of Oxford.
It furthers the University's objective of excellence in research, scholarship,
and education by publishing worldwide. Oxford is a registered trade mark of
Oxford University Press in the UK and certain other countries.

Published in the United States of America by Oxford University Press
198 Madison Avenue, New York, NY 10016, United States of America.

© 2021 by Oxford University Press

Library of Congress Cataloging-in-Publication Data

Names: Faunce, Kenneth V., 1962- author.
Title: Heavy traffic : the global drug trade in historical perspective /
  Ken Faunce, Washington State University.
Description: New York : Oxford University Press, [2021] | Series: Roots of
  contemporary issues | Includes bibliographical references and index. |
  Summary: "A higher education history book on the global drug trade"—
  Provided by publisher.
Identifiers: LCCN 2020025125 | ISBN 9780190696238 (paperback) | ISBN
  9780197542835 (epub) | ISBN 9780190696283
Subjects: LCSH: Drug traffic—History. | Drug abuse—History. | Drugs of
  abuse—History.
Classification: LCC HV5801 .F38 2021 | DDC 382/.456151—dc23
LC record available at https://lccn.loc.gov/2020025125

To my wife Karen,
for her loving support throughout
this project and for listening patiently to
all my trivia about drug history.

CONTENTS

LIST OF MAPS AND FIGURES

Maps

Figures

ABOUT THE AUTHOR

Ken Faunce is an Associate Professor (Career Track) of History at Washington State University. He spent years working for the federal government as a historian and archaeologist. His primary area of research is gender studies and race/ethnicity. He has done extensive research in the history of drugs and organized crime. He teaches such courses as Roots of Contemporary Issues, Drugs in World History, and Organized Crime in America. He has won numerous teaching awards, including the Richard Law Excellence in Undergraduate Teaching Award and the Martin Luther King Distinguished Service Award for Faculty at Washington State University.

ACKNOWLEDGMENTS

O ver the years in my classes, students regularly asked questions about the role of drugs in history. This prompted me to research the drug trade and its relationship to globalization, which led to this book. This volume would not have been possible without my colleagues in the Roots of Contemporary Issues Program at Washington State University. I want to thank Jesse Spohnholz, Clif Stratton, Sean Wempe, and Karen Phoenix for their help with resources, ideas on direction, and regular editing support. This volume would not have been possible without their help. I want to thank Julian Dodson for his help with Latin American history and Suzanna Reiss for our conversations on empire, which focused my ideas. I also want to thank the staff at the WSU library for all their help in finding the sources I needed, no matter how obscure. I would especially like to thank Jason Dormady, Central Washington University; Tara Dixon, Northeastern University; Jason Ripper, Everett Community College; James De Lorenzi, CUNY John Jay; Erin O'Donnell, East Stroudsburg University of Pennsylvania; Douglas T. McGetchin, Florida Atlantic University; W. Brian Newsome, Elizabethtown College; Marko Maunula, Clayton State University; Nicola Foote, Florida Gulf Coast University; Molly A. Warsh, University of Pittsburgh; Suzanna Reiss, University of Hawai'I Manoa, who reviewed the initial proposal and sample chapters; and especially Paul Gootenberg, Stony Brook University, who reviewed the entire manuscript. Their detailed comments and edits made this a stronger history. Finally, I would like to thank Charles Cavaliere, Danica Donovan, and other editors and staff at Oxford University Press for being helpful and supportive at every stage of the book's development.

Connecting Past and Present

Let's begin with events taking place in the last few years. Here's one: in early 2019, Starbucks announced plans to replace plastic straws with recyclable polypropylene lids. "Starbucks is finally drawing a line in the sand and creating a mold for other brands to follow," stated the company's director of packaging. Some supporters see the move as a good example of a market-based solution to environmental damage. Critics warn that it's unlikely that many "green" lids will end up at recycling facilities, since the plan is only slated for stores in two of the seventy-six countries where the company operates, the United States and Canada, which recycle very few polypropylene plastics. Most people agree, though, that plastic pollution has become a problem; worldwide production of plastics in the last few generations has skyrocketed. Many plastics produced today only ever get used for just a few minutes or hours, and then are left for centuries to pollute the earth. Plastics float in enormous masses in our oceans, killing birds, fish, seals, whales, and turtles. They break down into microplastics, making their way into all kinds of organisms. Microplastics found in drinking water are even changing humans' body chemistry. Whose responsibility is it to solve this problem? What solutions are likely to be effective? We will be in a better position to answer those questions if we stop to understand the economic, cultural, political, and social forces that allowed such widespread global plastic pollution to develop in the first place.

Here's another example: On January 28, 2019 the rapper 21 Savage sang a lyric on NBC's *Late Night with Jimmy Fallon* criticizing the US government's policy of separating children from parents who had arrived at the US–Mexico border seeking asylum. A few days later, the US Immigration and Customs Enforcement (ICE) arrested 21 Savage, just a week before the Grammy Awards, for which he had been nominated for his recent collaboration with Post Malone. It turns out the Atlanta-based musician had been brought to the US as a minor by his parents, who failed to renew his visa when it expired. During the Grammys, 21 Savage sat in an ICE detention facility. Supporters of 21 Savage applaud his bringing attention to what they consider an inhumane US immigration policy. Those who disagree with him emphasize the importance of protecting the integrity of national borders and prosecuting violations of American immigration laws. 21 Savage's case became part of a nationwide debate in the US about the arrival of asylum seekers fleeing gang violence in El Salvador, Guatemala, and Honduras, and the US government's policy of incarcerating children and separating them from their parents. Disagreements on this issue have overlapped with discussions about asylum-seekers from the Syrian Civil War, as well as about migrants from Latin America who come to the US to work, mostly in the agricultural and service industries, but do not get visas or overstay their visas. But questions about immigration policy and how to response to asylum-seekers are by no means limited to the US. In the last couple of years, politicians and ordinary people have been debating similar questions about immigration driven by persecution, poverty, fear of violence, and other hardships in countries such as Lebanon, Turkey, Germany, Britain, India, Bangladesh, Colombia, Brazil, Kenya, and Ethiopia. But too often political dialogue on these issues feels like everyone's goal is to convince others that they are wrong, and treat changing one's mind as a failure rather than as a success. As with the example of plastic, if we work to understand the historical factors that led to these situations, we'll be far better poised to solve problems effectively, instead of contributing to increased polarization.

Here's a third example: a man who murdered over fifty Muslim worshippers in Christchurch, New Zealand, in March 2019 was found to have been sharing white nationalist ideas with like-minded people on Facebook and Instagram in the run-up to his attack. It turns out that a man who murdered nine African Americans worshipping in a church in Charleston, South Carolina, four years earlier had also been using Facebook to exchange hateful and racist ideas with others. Certainly, social media has given people a new platform to spew hate speech, but is there really a relationship between increased racist violence and our new forms of digital communication? After the Christchurch killings, Facebook's executives decided that there was. They announced that the company would remove all white nationalist content from posts on Facebook and its subsidiary, Instagram. Supporters cheered that this massive social media company was taking responsibility to limit hate speech. Critics warned against limiting free speech online. Debate has also centered on whether private companies or governments should be responsible for regulating hate speech or protecting free speech. Meanwhile, others worry that extremists are only migrating to new venues, including to the dark web, where they can plot violence free of any oversight. At times one might feel paralyzed by the situation. We want to limit mass violence, but should we accept restrictions on our freedoms to do so? There are other important questions connected to this one. Should anyone be responsible for governing speech on social media? If so, who? And how should do they it? How else could we respond to incidents of mass violence? Often discussions on these topics are guided by people earning ad revenues for every click, offering easy-to-understand and frantically delivered messages. Fortunately, understanding the longer history of topics like censorship, racism, communication revolutions, and mass violence allows us to take a broader, more mature perspective. Rather than feeling paralyzed, studying the past allows us to make informed decisions about issues and leaves us empowered to help shape the future.

One last example. As the first volumes of this book series entered production in early 2020, a novel coronavirus, which causes the sometimes fatal respiratory illness known as COVID-19, was spreading rapidly throughout the world. First detected in Wuhan, China in late 2019, coronavirus spread to 183 countries and territories in a matter of months. By early April 2020 more than 73,000 people had died, with more than 1.3 million confirmed infections.

In response to this pandemic, national governments have taken uneven measures. South Korea aggressively tested, tracked, and treated in order to slow the spread of the disease. British Prime Minister Boris Johnson faced criticism for his government's more meager response. Johnson delayed the closure of schools, bars, restaurants, museums, and other common gathering spots, even as positive cases in the United Kingdom surpassed 1,300 in mid-March. By early April, Johnson himself landed in intensive care with COVID-19 symptoms.

While we do not yet know the long-term outcomes of the coronavirus pandemic, it has already begun to expose the degree to which the rapid circulation of goods and people throughout the world exposes us all to health threats, even if it does so unevenly. This novel coronavirus has revealed deep global inequities in access to medical care, adequate nutrition, and stable employment that make one more or less likely to contract and survive disease. It has left many societies caught up in a web of just-in-time supply chains woefully underprepared to combat the health threat. The pandemic has exposed the dangers of rapid global travel in spreading disease and highlighted humans' reliance on that same global transportation to share medical supplies and healthcare personnel. Many advocates of open borders around the world, for example, are supporting border closures to slow the spread of the disease. At least in April 2020, many politicians in the United States seem to be rapidly shifting their positions on policies related to incarceration, debt collection, healthcare, and guaranteed basic income. The pandemic has also raised important questions about the threats to public health from the intentional and unintentional spread of disinformation. In short order, coronavirus has made us all comprehend just how dependent we are on our fellow humans, for better and for worse. Coronavirus did not create the problems that it has exposed. A purely medical response to the disease will not solve those problems either. But understanding the historical origins of intertwined economic, political, and social developments that shape its spread will put all of us in a better position to address current and future problems rendered acute by disease.

It is the premise of this book series that understanding and addressing the aforementioned issues and others facing us today requires understanding their deep and global historical roots. Today's problems are not simply the outcomes of decisions yesterday—they are shaped by years, decades, and centuries of historical developments. A deep historical understanding helps us understand the present-day world in more sophisticated, mature, and reasoned ways. Humans have been interconnected with faraway places for centuries; solving the central problems facing our world means understanding those connections over time.

Too often our popular political dialogue—increasingly driven by social media, partisan politics, and short-term economic interests—ignores or discounts the complex historical dimensions of current issues and thus fails to provide useful contexts for those issues that could help citizens and leaders resolve them. Historians can help their fellow citizens make decisions by explaining the historical developments that created the world we inherited.

Rather than survey all of world history, each book in this series begins in the present with a pressing or seemingly intractable problem facing humanity (i.e., climate change, terrorism, racism, poverty). It then helps us better understand that not only is that problem not intractable, but it has historical origins. That is, it has not been a problem since time immemorial, nor is it unique to the present. Rather, problems have historical lives, have undergone changes both subtle and dramatic, and are the outcomes of human decisions and actions. The book in front of you and others in this series will help you: (1) understand the deep historical roots of a pressing and controversial issue facing the world today; (2) understand its global context; (3) interpret evidence to make reasoned, mature conclusions; (4) evaluate the arguments of others surrounding those issues; and (5) identify and utilize research skills to make independent conclusions about contemporary issues of interest to you.

The Case for the Roots of Contemporary Issues

Five central arguments shape this series' scope. First, every book explains why history matters now. Widespread consensus abounds that history helps individuals make reasonable decisions about the present and future. This is why so many governments require that their citizens study history. And yet, in the United States at least, history is pretty consistently among the least popular subjects for high school and college students. Why is this? The answer is probably in part because it is required and because we give so much attention in our society to prioritizing personal and short-term interests, such that studying history seems impractical. Books in this series are explicit about how essential, practical, and empowering studying history is.

Second, all books in the series offer world history, rather than histories of "civilizations" or continents. None of these books, for instance, stops at the history of the "West." There is a good reason for this: the very idea of the "West" only emerged as an effort to imagine a fundamental civilizational distinctiveness that has never existed. The "West" developed in response to interactions between people in Europe and North America with peoples around the world. The "West" offered a politically motivated myth of a linear inheritance from Greece and Rome to modern Europe, and from modern Europe to the United States. But many facts had to be omitted (intentionally or unintentionally) to sustain that argument.

The idea of the "West" had its core in some kind of definition of Europe, and tacked on the majority-white populations in settler colonies in North America, Australia, and elsewhere. That is, the definition of the "West" is rooted in ideas about race and in global racism, which were not just products of internal developments (i.e., developments taking place exclusively within Europe and the United States), but also of the centuries-long interactions of people around the globe, including systems of colonialism and slavery. In short, these volumes recognize that humans have interacted across large spaces for centuries, and that many of the geographical terms that we use to understand the world—the West, Middle East, the Far East, Europe, America, Africa—only came to exist as products of those interactions.

Third, while all volumes in the series offer world histories, they are also different from most world histories in that they focus on the history of a specific issue. In our view, a central challenge facing a lot of world history is the magnitude of coverage required by adopting a global scope. Some solve this problem by dividing up the world into continents. That approach can be effective, but suffers from the same challenge as books that adopt civilizational paradigms like "the West." Others attempt to solve the problem by adopting global narratives that replace older civilizational ones. A global approach can help us see patterns previously overlooked, but risk erasing the complexity of human experiences and decisions in order to tell universalizing stories that can make the outcomes look inevitable. They often do not capture the extent to which even major outcomes—political revolutions, technological changes, economic transformations—are the products of decisions made by ordinary people. Neither can they capture the logical counterpoint: that those people could have made other decisions, and that ordinary people actually do transform the world every day.

The fourth argument that shapes the scope of this series relates to the interconnection between premodern and modern history. What does "modern" signify in the first place? Most understandings of the past rely on this concept, but its meaning is notoriously hard to pin down. One easy way to think about the options is to look at how historians have divided up history into premodern and modern eras in textbooks and classes.

One common dividing point is 1500. The argument here is that a set of shifts between roughly 1450 and 1550 fundamentally transformed the world so that the periods after and before this period can be understood as distinct from one another. These include global explorations, the information revolution associated with the invention of the printing press, a set of military campaigns that established the boundaries of lands ruled by Muslim and Christian princes, and the spread of Renaissance capitalism.

Another common dividing point between the modern and premodern is 1800. Critical here are the development of industrial production and transportation, democratic forms of governance, waves of anti-colonial revolutions in the Americas, novel forms of Western imperialism that came to dominate much of Africa and Asia, the intensification of scientific understandings of the world, and the spread of new secular ideologies, like nationalism. There are other dividing points that historians have used to separate history, but these two are the most common.

Regardless of which breaking point you find most convincing, there are at least two problems with this way of dividing histories along "modern" and "premodern" lines. First, these divisions are usually Eurocentric in orientation. They presuppose that "modernity" was invented in Europe, and then exported elsewhere. As a result, peoples whose histories are divided up differently or that are less marked by European norms wrongly appear "backward." The second problem with these divisions is that they are less capable of identifying continuities across these divides.

We are not arguing that distinguishing between "modern" and "premodern" is always problematic. Rather, we see advantages to framing histories *across* these divides. Histories that only cover the modern period sometimes simplify the premodern world or treat people who lived long ago as irrelevant, often missing important early legacies. Meanwhile, histories that only cover premodern periods often suffer because their relevance for understanding the present is hard to see. They sometimes ask questions of interest to only professional historians with specialized knowledge. This series seeks to correct for each of these problems by looking for premodern inheritances in the modern world.

The final argument that shapes the series is that we have a stronger understanding of developments when we study the interrelationships between large structures of power, processes of change, and individual responses to both. The books work to help you understand how history has unfolded by examining the past from these three interactive perspectives. The first is structural: how political, economic, social, and, cultural power functioned at specific times and places. The second explains what forces have led to transformations from one condition to another. The third looks at how individuals have responded to both structures and changes, including how they resisted structures of power in ways that promoted change.

Historians distinguish between structure, change, and agency. Leaving out agency can make structures and changes look inevitable. Leaving out change flattens out the world, as if it were always the same (hint: always be skeptical of a sentence that begins with: "Throughout history"!). Leaving out structures celebrates human choices and autonomy, but naively ignores how broader contexts limit or shape our options. Understanding how structure, change, and agency interact allows us to create a more realistic picture of how the world works.

Doing History

When we talk to authors about writing these books, we urge that they do not need to provide all the answers to the issues that they write about, but should instead provide readers with the skills to find answers for themselves. That is, using the goals just described, this series is meant to help you think more critically about the relationship between the past and the present by developing discrete but mutually reinforcing research and analytical skills.

First, the volumes in this series will help you learn how to ask critical historical questions about contemporary issues—questions that do not beg simplistic answers but instead probe more deeply into the past, bridge seemingly disconnected geographies, and recognize the variety of human experiences. Second, you will learn how to assess, integrate, and compare the arguments of scholars who study both historical and contemporary issues. Historians do not always agree about cause and effect, the relative importance of certain contributing factors over others, or even how best to interpret a single document. This series will help you understand the importance of these debates and to find your own voice within them.

Third, you will learn how to identify, evaluate, interpret, and organize varieties of primary sources—evidence that comes from the periods you are studying—related to specific historical processes. Primary sources are the raw evidence contained in the historical record, produced at the time of an event or process either by a person or group of people directly involved or by a first-hand observer. Primary sources nearly always require historians to analyze and present their larger significance. As such, you will learn how to develop appropriate historical contexts within which to situate primary sources.

While we listed these three sets of skills in order, in fact you might begin with any one of them. For example, you may already have a historical question in mind after reading several recent news articles about a contemporary problem. That question would allow you to begin searching for appropriate debates about the historical origins of that problem or to seek out primary sources for analysis. Conversely, you might begin searching for primary sources on a topic of interest to you and then use those primary sources to frame your question. Likewise, you may start with an understanding of two opposing viewpoints about the historical origins of the problem and then conduct your own investigation into the evidence to determine which viewpoint ultimately holds up.

But only after you have developed each of these skills will you be in a position to practice a fourth critical skill: producing analytical arguments backed by historical evidence and situated within appropriate scholarly debates and historical contexts. Posing such arguments will allow you to make reasoned, mature conclusions about how history helps us all address societal problems with that same reason and maturity. We have asked authors to model and at times talk through these skills as they pertain to the issue they have contributed to the series.

Series Organization

Each volume in this series falls under one of five primary themes in history. None attempt to offer a comprehensive treatment of all facets of a theme, but instead will expose you to more specific and focused histories and questions clearly relevant to understanding the past's impact on the present.

The first theme—Humans and the Environment—investigates how we have interacted with the natural world over time. It considers how the environment shapes human life, but also how humans have impacted the environment by examining economic, social, cultural, and political developments. The second theme, Globalization, allows us to put our relationship to the natural world into a greater sense of motion. It explores the transformations that have occurred as human relationships have developed across vast distances over centuries. The third theme, the Roots of Inequality, explores the great disparities (the "haves" and "have-nots") of the world around us, along lines of race, gender, class, or other differences. This approach allows us to ask questions about the origins of inequality, and how the inequalities in the world today relate to earlier eras, including the past five hundred years of globalization.

Diverse Ways of Thinking, the fourth theme, helps us understand the past's diverse peoples on their own terms and to get a sense of how they understood one another and the world around them. It addresses the historical nature of ideologies and worldviews that people have developed to conceptualize the differences and inequalities addressed in the inequality theme. The fifth theme, the Roots of Contemporary Conflicts, explores the historical roots of conflicts rooted in diverse worldviews, environmental change, inequalities, and global interactions over time. Its goal is to illuminate the global and local factors that help explain specific conflicts. It often integrates elements of the previous four themes within a set of case studies rooted in the past but also helps explain the dramatic changes we experience and/or witness in the present.

Our thematic organization is meant to provide coherence and structure to a series intended to keep up with global developments in the present as historians work to provide essential contexts for making sense of those developments. Every subject facing the world today—from responding to COVID-19 to debates about the death penalty, from transgender rights to coal production, and from the Boko Haram rebellion in Nigeria to micro-aggressions in Massachusetts—can be better understood by considering the topic in the context of world history.

History is not a path toward easy solutions: we cannot simply copy the recommendations of Mohandas Gandhi, Sojourner Truth, Karl Marx, Ibn Rushd, or anyone else for that matter, to solve problems today. To do so would be foolhardy. But we can better understand the complex nature of the problems we face so that the solutions we develop are mature, responsible, thoughtful, and informed. In the following book, we have asked one historian with specialized knowledge and training in this approach to guide you through this process for one specific urgent issue facing the world.

—Jesse Spohnholz and Clif Stratton

ROOTS OF CONTEMPORARY ISSUES

HEAVY TRAFFIC

INTRODUCTION

The Globalization of Drugs

It's not peace instead of war, it's a more intelligent way to fight . . . the use of drugs. Stop
the war on drugs and let's be more constructive in trying to reduce consumption. We cannot
have one recipe. It's not so easy to say stop the war on drugs and let's legalize, it's more
complicated than that, between prohibition and legalization there is an enormous variety of
solutions in between.

—FERNANDO HENRIQUE CARDOSO,
The Global Commission on Drug Policy 2011[1]

The United Nations Office on Drugs and Crime's (UNODC) findings in the
2018 World Drug Report demonstrate that both the variety of drugs and
drug markets are expanding and diversifying.[2] The UNODC argues that the international community needs to increase its responses to cope with these challenges.
One aspect of the expansion of global markets today is the increasing supply.
Manufacturers are producing opium and cocaine, legally and illegally, at higher
levels than ever before. Every day we read new media reports detailing the growing opioid crisis in North America, which clearly demonstrates the extent of the
problem.

In May 2019 Johnson & Johnson, one of the world's largest drug manufacturers, went on trial in a multibillion dollar lawsuit brought by the state
of Oklahoma. Prosecutors accuse the firm of deceptively marketing painkillers and downplaying addiction risks, fueling an "opioid epidemic."[3] Johnson &
Johnson denied wrongdoing, stating that the company marketed products

---

1. Quoted in Michelle Nichols, "Global War on Drugs a Failure, High-Level Panel Says,"
Health News, June 2, 2011, https://www.reuters.com/article/us-drugs-commission/global-war-
on-drugs-a-failure-high-level-panel-says-idUSTRE7513XW20110602.

2. United Nations Office on Drugs and Crime, *World Drug Report: Executive Summary
Conclusions and Policy Implications*. (United Nations: 2018), https://www.unodc.org/wdr2018/
prelaunch/WDR18_Booklet_1_EXSUM.pdf, 1.

3. Sean Murphy, "Oklahoma Attorney Blames Corporate Greed for Opioid Crisis," *AP News,*
May 28, 2019, https://www.apnews.com/616ef7ba545e4e5287e406182126938d.

responsibly. This will be the first litigated case of the 2,000 claims brought by state, local, and tribal governments against pharmaceutical firms in the United States—an indication that nonmedical use of prescription drugs has reached epidemic proportions in the country. This is also true for other parts of the world.

Global markets for cocaine have extended beyond their usual regions and drug trafficking continues to grow rapidly, despite efforts by governments around the world, including the United States' "war on drugs." Most experts agree that the global war on drugs—based on the United States' highly punitive and often moralistic approach—has failed.[4] Most of the world's cocaine comes from producers in Colombia, who boosted manufacturing by more than one-third from 2015 to 2016 due to the increase in global sales.[5] Another example of this can be seen in South Korea, where cocaine producers are using the country as a gateway to China and the rest of Asia.

In December 2018, South Korea custom officials seized over 168 million dollars' worth of cocaine in the southern port of Busan.[6] The shipment was en route to Mainland China for distribution across the country. The South Korea government, which has very strict laws against recreational drug use, is concerned that South American, Japanese, and Taiwanese drug cartels are trying to make South Korea into the new Asian shipping point for illegal drugs. There is an increasing demand by consumers for cocaine in the Asian market, and South Korea could become the new transportation hub for cocaine as well as other illegal drugs. The increasing demand in the global market is affecting not only cocaine and opium production but that of other types of drugs as well.

While cocaine and opium seem to dominate the popular headlines at times, these two drugs are not the only ones to have an impact on the global market. The market in coffee, tobacco, and alcohol, also part of the international trade routes, is having an effect on economies and societies around the world. The production of these legal substances continues at a steady pace. We can see the impact on global trade by highlighting coffee in Brazil, alcohol in South Africa, and tobacco in Turkey.

---

4. Ethan Nadelmann, "The Failure of the War on Drugs: An Overview," in *Global Viewpoints: Drugs*, ed. Maria Tenaglia-Webster (Detroit: Gale Cengage, 2009), 27.

5. UNODC, *World Drug Report*, June 2018, https://www.unodc.org/wdr2018/prelaunch/WDR18_Booklet_1_EXSUM.pdf, 9.

6. Josh Doyle, "US$168 Million Cocaine Haul Sparks Fears South Korea Becoming ateway to China, Rest of Asia," *South China Morning Post*, December 18, 2018, https://www.scmp.com/news/asia/east-asia/article/2178570/us168-million-cocaine-haul-sparks-fears-south-korea-becoming.

In 2018, Brazil had a bumper crop of more than 60 million bags of coffee. Global coffee output in 2018–2019 has the potential to be over 170 million bags, which is 10 million more than current consumption.[7]

What does this mean for coffee prices? Due to the expected overproduction prices have dropped, which has weakened the economy of major coffee exporters like Brazil. While this drop in prices could be a boon for consumers, Brazilian farmers are now operating on a thin profit margin. Many coffee farmers cannot pay their debts and have been forced to sell their land.[8] Changes in global markets often have detrimental effects on local producers.

The World Health Organization ranks South Africa sixth globally in alcohol consumption.[9] Alcohol sales in South Africa reached 106 billion per year in 2016, and was projected to reach 129 billion in 2019.[10] While the majority of alcohol consumed is produced in South Africa, it is produced by subsidiaries of foreign alcohol manufacturers, with one of the largest being Newco, formed out of a merger between South African Breweries (SABMiller) and Anheuser-Busch InBev (AB InBev) in 2016.[11] The cost of this increase in drinking has led to rising levels of alcoholism, increasing health costs, and drunk driving incidents in South Africa.[12] High alcohol consumption in the country has roots in the colonial system, where laborers received cheap wine as part of their daily wages. In this case the spread of alcohol can be linked to imperialism, which is a major process in globalization.

In Turkey the global trade in tobacco is making news. Transnational tobacco companies (TTCs) entered the cigarette market in Turkey in the 1980s due

7. Jos Algra, "The 2018 Coffee Price Crisis: Market Fundamentals and the Human Cost," *Daily Coffee News,* September 19, 2018, https://dailycoffeenews.com/2018/09/19/the-2018-coffee-price-crisis-market-fundamentals-and-the-human-cost/.

8. Algra, "The 2018 Coffee Price Crisis."

9. Grieve Chelwa and Corné Van Walbeek, "SA Ranks Sixth Globally as a Nation of Drinkers," *Business Day,* March 4, 2019, https://www.businesslive.co.za/bd/opinion/2019-03-04-sa-ranks-sixth-globally-as-a-nation-of-drinkers/.

10. "The South African Liquor Industry, 2018," *Research and Markets (Global Newswire),* January 31, 2019, https://www.globenewswire.com/news-release/2019/01/31/1708601/0/en/The-South-African-Liquor-Industry-2018-Growth-is-Expected-in-2018-Despite-the-Poor-Economic-Climate-and-Will-Be-Aided-by-Currency-Weakness-Reflected-in-Rising-Exports.html.

11. Nina Shand, "The Liquor Industry: South Africa," *African Business Information,* September 13, 2017, https://www.whoownswhom.co.za/store/info/4533?segment=The+Liquor+Industry.

12. Kealeboga Mokolobate, "Effects of Alcohol Consumption in South Africa: From Cradle to Grave," *Mail & Guardian,* October 27, 2017, https://mg.co.za/article/2017-10-27-00-effects-of-alcohol-consumption-in-south-africa-from-the-cradle-to-the-grave.

to the loosening of trade and investment restrictions.[13] This change was made under the oversight of the International Monetary Fund (IMF), the World Bank, and the World Trade Organization (WTO), which are all global economic institutions. The TTCs increased tobacco sales through massive advertising, foreign investment, and lobbying of the Turkish government. Three major companies, Philip Morris, British American Tobacco, and Japan Tobacco, dominate the market in Turkey. Anti-tobacco advocates have tried to limit smoking in Turkey, but due to the political and economic influence of the TTCs they have made little progress. The numbers of smokers rose to 15.7 million in 2015 and has not changed in the last few years.[14] This increase in smoking is causing health costs in the country to rise, but due to the influences of global companies and organizations, anti-tobacco efforts have gained little traction.

As we can see from these examples, the international trade in these drugs has a significant impact on the economies and societies in countries around the world. These drugs not only make up a significant portion of these countries' economy, but the impact of health risks and illegal activities is taking its toll. How did this international market for drugs develop? What roles have merchants, government officials, and drug manufacturers played in shaping this market over time and space? What can this tell us about the process of globalization?

By examining the history of the global drug trade, this book offers insight into globalization as an historical process, thereby helping to make sense of today's interconnected world where products grown or produced in only a handful of places circulate widely, with varying impacts on local populations. By investigating how producers, merchants, consumers, laborers, and government officials have created, sustained, transformed, and at times sought to destroy this global drug market, we can begin to understand globalization not as an inevitable or natural process, but instead as one that is created by and responds to a variety of human motivations. Globalization has resulted in a growing interdependence of the world's economies, cultures, and populations. To understand this process, we need to define the process of globalization.

The term "globalization" is often used by scholars to describe a variety of economic, political, social, and cultural changes.[15] While a common popular perception is that globalization is a modern phenomenon linked to the creation of the internet, most historians dispute this idea. Long before globalization became a popular term, historians studied the emergence and continued integration of

---

13. "Anti-Tobacco Control Industry Strategies in Turkey," *BMC Public Health,* February 26, 2018, https://bmcpublichealth.biomedcentral.com/articles/10.1186/s12889-018-5071-z.

14. Osman Elbek, Efza Evrengil, Elif Dagli, Fusun Yildiz, Murat Güner, and Tanzer Gezer, "Sustaining Tobacco Control Success: A Challenge for Turkey," *European Respiratory Journal* (2017): 50, https://erj.ersjournals.com/content/50/suppl_61/PA2660.

15. Shalmali Guttal, "Globalisation," *Development in Practice* 17, no. 4/5 (August 2007): 523.

the global economy, which they argue appeared in the fifteenth and sixteenth centuries.[16] Debates about globalization include how to define it, the central actors, driving forces, and origins. Many scholars agree that integration is brought about by cross-border trade in goods and services, changes in technology, and flows of investment, people, and information.[17] However, globalization is not only defined by capitalist economic expansion. This common use of the term sometimes wrongly makes globalization seem like an inevitable process of invisible market forces. But as we will see, globalization is also about political participation and imperial conquest, the spread (and sometimes imposition) of cultural values, and the movement of peoples. The processes of economic integration are fundamentally shaped by political processes of conquest and cooperation and by coercive and cooperative forms of cultural and ideological exchange. The wide-ranging effects of globalization are complex and can be politically charged. Globalization can benefit societies, but also can be harmful to individuals and societies.[18] Political, cultural, and ideological decisions help drive the process, demonstrating that globalization is not inevitable. Acknowledging multiple influences also forces us to stop using the term as if it were one single, unifying process. For this volume we will focus on the process of globalization through the lens of the drug trade.

Why drugs? The choices made by producers, merchants, reformers, and government officials highlights key features of the process of globalization. Drugs became a global commodity due to the decisions made by producers and merchants looking for a commodity desired by consumers. The Industrial Revolution, mass production, and commercialization aided in increasing the drug market. Choices made by government officials to increase their country's economic and political power during the spread of imperialism supported the drug market. Cultural imperialism pushed by Western government officials and reformers helped create an illegal market for some types of drugs. Finally, actions and decisions made by government officials and by the collapse of the old imperial powers during the Cold War impacted the drug trade, which illustrates changes in globalization in the post–World War II world.

Critics might suggest that other commodities experienced these same processes as they became part of the global market. What part of the drug trade makes it different than other commodities? One main difference is that most other products on the global market do not have an addictive quality. The varying levels of addiction allows for this aspect of globalization to have deeper, and at times more intense, impacts. While drug addiction was not the only factor

---

16. Jürgen Osterhammel and Niels P. Petersson, *Globalization: A Short History* (Princeton, NJ: Princeton University Press, 2005), 3.

17. Mark Kesselman, *The Politics of Globalization: A Reader* (Boston: Houghton Mifflin Company, 2007), 3–4.

18. Kesselman, *The Politics of Globalization*, 10.

in the spread of drugs, it did aid in making them global commodities. Drugs also became a part of cultural taboos, colonial conquests, and the exploitation of workers.

At this point I need to define what I mean by "drugs." A drug is any substance that changes an organism's physiology or psychology when consumed, excluding food or water. The legality of specific drugs has changed depending on time period or location. As we will see, many drug markets began without regulation and became well established before reformers, fearing addiction or social harm, promoted prohibition. These prohibited drugs then became part of an illegal market. There are a wide variety of drugs produced and consumed around the world, but for this volume I will focus on coffee (caffeine), tobacco, rum, opium, and cocaine. The analysis of these five drugs provide insight into various aspects of the global drug trade and the historical process of globalization. Using these five drugs, we can examine the Indian Ocean and Atlantic Ocean trade; the role of industrialization and imperialism; attempts at prohibition, which created the illegal market; and the changes brought on by the Cold War. The development of the international market for these drugs highlights the political, economic, and cultural facets of globalization, providing us with a better understanding of how the process changed over time leading to the creation of the modern world.

Structure

While the exact beginning of globalization is debated, we begin the discussion in the sixteenth century. This book is organized into five chapters that examine the development of the global drug trade. Chapter 1 covers the sixteenth through eighteenth centuries, while chapters 2 and 3 examine the processes of globalization in the nineteenth century by exploring different dimensions of the process. Chapter 4 moves from the nineteenth century into the early twentieth century, and chapter 5 covers the late twentieth century. While these chapters are organized chronologically, they each focus on five processes supporting the spread of globalization: maritime trade, industrialization, imperialism (including cultural imperialism), Cold War empires, and decolonization.

Chapter 1 examines the beginnings of globalization with oceangoing trade in the fifteenth and sixteenth century. The chapter highlights the change from local and regional trade networks to early international trade. The first example is the Indian Ocean trade in coffee, which started with production in Mocha, a trade city on the southwest tip of Arabian Peninsula, and developed the beverage as a major commodity by the sixteenth century across Arabia and Africa and then to Europe. The chapter then shifts its focus to the Atlantic Ocean tobacco trade, which spread from the North American colonies to Europe and Asia. The last example, rum, traveled with merchant ships as supplies for the sailors, from the Caribbean to Africa and Asia by the eighteenth century, thereby creating a global market. The trade in each of these drugs started locally and became fully global by the eighteenth century. As we examine the spread of the trade in coffee, tobacco, and rum, I will focus the discussion on the actions and decisions made by producers, merchants, and consumers to gain an understanding of the process of early globalization. Slavery and the Atlantic slave trade played a major role in the production of these three drugs starting in the sixteenth century. The chapter will also explore the changes in the global drug business as European merchants started to dominate trade and production by the eighteenth century.

The industrialization and commercialization of drugs in the nineteenth century—the focus of chapter 2 — explores how the mass production of commodities intensified the global connections begun in the fifteenth century. The Industrial Revolution was one of the major drivers of globalization during the nineteenth century. A wide variety of choices, decisions, and processes drove the mass production and mass consumption of drugs. This chapter focuses on the industrialization and commercialization of opium and cocaine during the Industrial Revolution. I start with the growing medical consensus that opium offered a cure for a wide variety of problems. The chapter then moves to an examination of the spread of opium from India into China, with a focus on the East India Company. It will discuss the impact and spread of opium in Asia and its relationship to the trade in tea. I will then describe the development of morphine and heroin in the nineteenth century and the spread of laudanum in patent medicines. The chapter also explores the development and production of cocaine in the nineteenth century as a new "wonder drug." Both drugs became mass-produced commodities due to industrialization, but opium and cocaine also became global commodities because of commercialization and advertising, which sheds light on the process of globalization.

Chapter 3 also covers the global drug trade in the nineteenth century, but focuses on its relationship to imperialism and the cultural and racial implications of the drug trade. Imperialism was another of the major drivers behind the spread of globalization, which this chapter explores in relation to coffee, rum, and tobacco. This includes the spread of coffee colonies in Ceylon (present-day Sri Lanka) and Indonesia, tobacco production in the Caribbean, and rum production in Asia and Africa. The chapter also expands on the importation of opium in China and growing imperialism in Asia, including the Opium Wars and the movement of poppy production from India to China. This chapter compares the impacts of imperialism in the cocaine market in Peru with that of opium in Asia. Chapter 3 is linked with chapter 2, as industrialization and imperialism are fully intertwined. Both of these processes are major driving forces in the spread of globalization.

Anti-drug movements and attempts to reform empires that emerged in the late nineteenth and early twentieth century will be the focus of chapter 4. It begins with an examination of the changing attitude toward opiates and cocaine in the nineteenth century, and the fear of rising levels of addiction. I will then move to the rise of temperance movements and the changing attitude toward alcohol. These movements represent the "civilizing mission" of reformers within the Western imperial powers. Reformers in the West believed they had a moral imperative to protect the indigenous populations from drugs in the colonies controlled by Europeans and Americans around the world. The chapter then turns to the movement to outlaw opiates and cocaine in the early twentieth century, which was strongly influenced by ideas about race that had been developing in recent decades. I will then use the prohibition of alcohol as an example of the attempt and failure of an anti-drug movement. The process of reform is a part of imperialism, and prohibition and reform are features of the spread of globalization.

Chapter 5 examines the relationship between the Cold War and the global drug trade in the late twentieth century and the emergence of the United States and the Soviet Union as major global players. The Cold War was a major contributor to modern globalization. I will start with an examination of Cold War politics and connections in relation to both legal and illegal drugs during the 1950s. The chapter then moves to the 1960s and 1970s, using the American war in Vietnam as an example of the growing global drug trade and its connection to Cold War actions. The United States waged its global war on drugs—started during the Nixon administration—by claiming to protect the world from certain drugs. Actually, one of the underlying reasons for the war on drugs was tied to US efforts to limit Communism and the influence of the Soviet Union, while increasing American influence around the world. The struggle between the two Cold War empires and their allies had a major effect on the global drug trade. Another dimension in this struggle is the decolonization movements that occurred as the old empires collapsed. The chapter closes with a look at free trade agreements and global capitalism in the 1990s, which are involved in rise of new global drug cartels and drug wars that still continue today.

Drugs are fully woven into our globalized society, leading to far ranging impacts. Understanding the social and political causes is necessary to understanding our world today. The history of the globalization of drugs provides a deeper understanding of the choices and decisions made by governments, organizations, and individuals leading to the role of drugs in the economy, politics, and society of the modern world.

Choices and Sources

Drugs of all varieties make up a major portion of our economy and our lives. These substances provide relief from pain, aid in medical treatment, and provide pleasure and escape. They also fuel addiction and related social problems. Drugs also provide us with an insight into the workings of global capitalist trade, as well as the choices made by individuals and organizations around the world. Globalization is a wide-ranging and complicated topic, and the trade in drugs reflects this complexity. Drugs have helped shaped politics, economies, and society since the Paleolithic era, which makes them a fascinating topic of research. While drugs have always been part of human society, my focus is on how drugs became part of a global market, which aids us in understanding the various processes of globalization.

Even focusing on the role of drugs in globalization is a daunting endeavor. Focusing on the development of globalization allowed me to narrow the scope to the sixteenth century for the start of this story. For this volume I had to make choices about which areas of the world to examine and which drugs to focus on. I decided that caffeine (coffee), tobacco, alcohol, cocaine, and opium provided the best examples of the development of globalization, as they provide key insights into political, economic, and cultural aspects of globalization. These five drugs are similar in how they became global commodities and by examining them, we can see how the decisions made by producers, consumers, government officials, and reformers shaped the global landscape.

The decision about what to include means that it was not possible to examine every region of the world. While drugs have impacted most areas of the world, it was impossible to discuss everything. Many regions of the world received less attention, but this does not mean they are any less important. This volume provides you with the analytical tools to select your own examples for further research. For example, you could explore in more depth the role of coffee in Central and South America, or the how the Chinese tobacco market developed. Other research opportunities include cocaine production in Cuba or Brazil, the opium trade in East Africa, or alcohol marketing in Japan. The role of illegal drugs and the development of organized crime around the world starting in the 1920s also deserves more attention.

Writing the history of the global drug trade—or any history—means making choices about sources and evidence. I relied on the work of fellow historians who studied the history of these drugs in more local, regional, or national contexts. These books and articles can be found throughout this volume in the footnotes and in the further reading section in each chapter. I relied on this thorough research and expertise to complete this volume. When searching for various titles on the history of drugs in the library stacks, I also examined the books surrounding the volume I was seeking. This allowed me to find several more titles, and I recommend you using this technique too, as it allows you to discover more sources for your research.

Secondary sources (later interpretations by scholars) can provide information, insights, and different ways to look at the issues. I used library search engines including JSTOR, Project Muse, and Google Books to locate useful sources. Secondary sources are useful and necessary for historical research. However, primary sources are the foundational evidence of history, the historical support for all those secondary source interpretations. To locate primary sources, I relied on a variety of organizational archives and databases, such as The Making of the Modern World and Academic Search Complete. Finding primary sources can be difficult as it involves time and patience, and occasional frustrations. However, the valuable information these sources provide is necessary to understanding your topic. The primary sources I analyzed in this volume do not represent all the historical evidence on the subject. The examination of these sources provides you, the reader, with examples in order to conduct your own research. Understanding globalization in historical perspective through the lens of the global drug trade not only provides insight into the process of globalization, but allows for you to practice source-gathering and develop analytical skills needed for any research project. Researching the role of drugs in globalization is a fascinating and informative way to understand the modern world.

1   DRUGS AND EARLY MODERN GLOBALIZATION

In 1698 Edward Ward, a satirical English writer, frequented London coffeehouses on a regular basis. Ward, the landlord of the King's Head Tavern, wrote about daily life in London at the end of the seventeenth century, and he described one of the favorite haunts:

> There was a rabble going hither and thither, reminding me of a swarm of rats in a ruinous cheese-store. Some came, others went; some were scribbling, others were talking; some were drinking coffee, some smoking, and some arguing; the whole place stank of tobacco like the cabin of a barge. On the corner of a long table, close by the armchair, was lying a Bible. Beside it were earthenware pitchers, long clay pipes, a little fire on the hearth, and over it the high coffee pot. Beneath a small bookshelf, on which were bottles, cups, and an advertisement for a beauti-fier to improve the complexion, was hanging a parliamentary ordinance against drinking and the use of bad language. The walls were decorated with gilt frames, much as a smithy is deco-rated with horseshoes. In the frames were rarities; phials of a yellowish elixir, favourite pills and hair tonics, packets of snuff, tooth powder made from coffee grounds, caramels and cough lozenges. Had not my friend told me that he had brought me to a coffee-house, I would have regarded the place as the big booth of a cheap-jack.[1]

What can we learn from his description of an early coffeehouse? How did drugs become global commodities? The expansion of oceangoing commerce served as a central driver of globalization, and the increase in the trade in drugs constitutes a critical facet of this global process. By focusing on the deliberate profit-driven spread of spirits, tobacco, coffee, and other drugs, we have the opportunity to see how global exchange of these drugs transformed the everyday lives of millions of people, as well as the natural environment. Today, many coffeehouse

---

1. Edward Ward, *The London Spy* (London: Printed for J. Nutt, near Stationers-Hall, 1698), 12.

visitors come to work or to meet with a small group of friends—paying for their beverages and settling into a nice quiet corner. If a seventeenth-century Londoner like Edward Ward walked into a coffee shop today, he may not even recognize this scene. Instead of paying for drinks, people in the seventeenth century paid a penny to enter a coffeehouse. Once inside, the patron could access coffee, tobacco, pamphlets, bulletins, newspapers, the company of other customers, and news "reporters."

These reporters or "runners" traveled around the coffeehouses announcing the latest news. Ward's coffeehouse description demonstrates the availability and mixing of two newly globalized commodities: coffee and tobacco. Coffeehouses also gave men like Ward an alternative to the third globalized product, rum. An eclectic group of people visited coffeehouses, and in a society where class and economical status dominated, people of all levels gathered together.[2] Shop owners, merchants, students, workers, and scholars gathered to discuss politics, literature, and religion. It is easy to imagine the wide range of ideas produced as a result of this intermingling of people. Coffeehouses encouraged open thought and gathering of community while profiting from drugs, like coffee and tobacco, from around the world.

We begin this examination with proto-globalization, which historians argue appeared between 1500 and 1800. First coined in 2003 by historians A. G. Hopkins and Christopher Bayly, the term "proto-globalization" describes the increasing economic and cultural exchanges that occurred in the period after the arrival of European colonizers and African slaves in the Americas, but before the Industrial Revolution—which began in the late eighteenth and early nineteenth century.[3] The period is often marked by the economic ascent of Western Europe, and the rise of larger-scale conflicts between powerful empires. We also see an intensification in the exchange of commodities including slaves, cotton, minerals, and drugs. Similar to many other commodities, the buying, selling, distribution, and exchange of drugs, while a set of economic transactions, also consisted of a process that shaped and was shaped by wider social and cultural contexts. Indeed, because the drug trade has been embedded in nearly every aspect of globalization, an exploration of the drug trade offers us a more careful understanding of the often vaguely defined process we call globalization.

This chapter examines proto-globalization by looking at three drug commodities during the early modern period: coffee, tobacco, and rum. The high demand

2. William B. Boulton, *The Amusements of Old London* (London: Ballantyne, Hanson & Co., 1901), 163.

3. A. G. Hopkins, ed., *Globalization in World History* (New York: Norton, 2003), 3. Christopher Bayly, *The Birth of the Modern World: Global Connections and Comparisons, 1780–1914*, (Hoboken, NJ: Wiley-Blackwell, 2004), 15.

for these commodities today might make their exchange and consumption seem inevitable. Due to their addictive nature, or at least stimulating qualities, demand increased or remained high and insured their continued circulation through global markets, or so the story goes. However, the story is not so simple. As we will see, demand alone does not drive or fully explain the global drug trade during the early modern period, or any other period for that matter.

Real understanding requires an investigation into the social, political, and economic forces that shaped the outcomes of the drug trade. The histories of these drugs reveal a series of choices and decisions made by all those involved that were far from predetermined. Indeed, it was the choices, decisions, and actions of individuals and groups that resulted in the expansion of the global drug trade, not just simple supply and demand or some inherent chemical qualities in the drugs themselves. What really made these three drugs popular? What choices did merchants and consumers make that led to the early globalization of these products? What impact did these drugs have on politics, religion, and society and vice versa? How and why did certain interests seek to repress or regulate the circulation and consumption of coffee, tobacco, and rum? How effective were those efforts? In order to understand the process of globalization we need to address these questions and to examine the contingency that produced a global drug trade in the forms that it took. In the sixteenth century, coffee, tobacco, and rum were part of regional trade networks. By the eighteenth century, these networks had become global. This chapter explores the decisions and actions that drove that process.

Coffee: An Indian Ocean History

The Bayans, a family of Muslim merchants from the Gujarati region of today's Pakistan, migrated to the city of Mocha, in the Muslim-dominated region of Yemen on the Arabian Peninsula, in the early sixteenth century. They rose in prominence in the Ottoman Empire, which ruled over the Arabian Peninsula, and became the most powerful and influential of the Mocha merchants. The Bayans tapped into an already emerging coffee trade and developed extensive credit networks, funding Yemeni coffee plantations. Their activities were remarkably successful: the family dominated the Indian Ocean coffee trade for a century and a half.[4] Using their coffee profits, the Bayans traded other lucrative commodities, including spices, silk, and textiles. The family became key operators

---

4. Jonathan Morris, "Coffeehouse Formats through the Centuries: Third Places or Public Spaces?" in *Coffee: A Comprehensive Guide to the Bean, the Beverage, and the Industry,* ed. Robert W. Thurston, Jonathan Morris, and Shawn Steiman (London: Rowman & Littlefield, 2013), 216.

in a vast Indian Ocean trade network that connected East Africa, Arabia, India, China, and Southeast Asia. The history of the Bayans and their sprawling coffee empire is in many respects indicative of the kind of decisions and actions that forged a global trade in drugs and other commodities during the early modern period. Indeed, that an immigrant family from northwestern India could come to dominate the Yemeni coffee trade in a state ruled by Ottoman Turks is rather remarkable from our twenty-first-century vantage point, when border crossing and immigrant labor is often highly regulated by nation-states.

But the Bayans and coffee, the main commodity they traded, also offer a much-needed fresh case study of *who* exactly drove proto-globalization between 1500 and 1800. Between the 1960s and the 1990s, historical research on the Indian Ocean economy focused primarily on the influence of European trading empires in Asia, including those of the Portuguese and the Dutch. This focus arose from an attempt to understand the reasons for the later rise of European power.[5] While this scholarship work was not entirely flawed, historians have since come to appreciate the extent to which the commercial activities of non-Europeans like the Bayans actually fueled early stages of the process we call globalization. While the trade was not yet fully global, the Indian Ocean was the heart of a trading system that connected East Asia, South Asia, East Africa, and Europe. Coffee was an important component of this complex system of international trade well before the arrival and certainly before the dominance of Europeans in the Indian Ocean system. By the time Europeans tapped directly into these networks, Arab, African, and Indian merchants had long negotiated and established its terms of exchange.

The rise of coffee within the Indian Ocean world was not just an outcome of economic forces. Its spread in the early modern era cannot be understood outside of its role with Islam, one of the most influential systems of religious thought within this trade network. Coffee, which seems to have originated in present-day Ethiopia, was first cultivated in the fourteenth century in Mocha a full century before the first Europeans arrived on the scene and even longer before the arrival of the Bayans.[6] Though a stimulant, Muslims did not consider coffee a drug, and many embraced it as a social agent and as an alternative to alcohol, which Islam prohibited. The appeal of coffee drinking outside of Mocha was due not only to the Islamic prohibition on alcohol but also in large part to the efforts of a broader Islamic mystic movement called Sufism, which rapidly spread from the twelfth century through missionary activity beyond lands where Arabic was the

5. Rila Mukherjee, "The Indian Ocean: Historians Writing History," *Asian Review of World Histories* 1, no. 2 (July 2013): 297.

6. David Courtwright, *Forces of Habit: Drugs and the Making of the Modern World* (Cambridge, MA: Harvard University Press, 2001), 19.

dominate language. Sufis stressed the transmission of Islamic knowledge through teaching and interpersonal exchange rather than through the literal reading of Islamic texts. This highly adaptable form of Islam lent itself to the incorporation of social practices, like coffee drinking, not addressed in official Islamic doctrine and to those practices found beyond the political control of Muslim rulers.

Sufis began to drink coffee on a regular basis by the late fifteenth century. The drug came to play a major role in Sufi religious practice because it allowed devotees to stay alert during nighttime rituals. Sufis came to believe that the roasting of the coffee bean, which transformed it from a simple bean into a stimulating beverage, symbolized the transformation of the soul: the passage of the divine light from the teacher's heart to the student's heart that allowed one to live closer to God. Coffee became the beverage of choice in most Sufi boarding schools, and Sufis used it as part of martial arts training regimens. In 1414, Sufis introduced coffee to the city of Mecca, the epicenter of Islamic religious pilgrimage, and the drink's popularity with non-Sufi Muslims increased over the next few decades. Men gathered at coffeehouses to discuss politics, religion, business, and social issues—activities that occurred beyond the prying eyes and ears of religious and government authorities. Consumers made deliberate choices to use the beverage to motivate social encounters, as they believed coffee, unlike alcohol, stimulated thought and conversation.

This embrace of what we could call a social coffee culture, and coffee's use as an integral part of Sufi religious ritual, was not without its critics and challengers. Since Sufis did not recognize orthodox Islamic or political authority, local Arab officials saw Sufism as a political threat. Many attempted to ban urban coffeehouses in order to stem the spread of Sufism.[7] Authorities also perceived the gathering of men to discuss the issues of the day as subversive behavior. Indeed, many coffee drinkers questioned or criticized the status quo. Critics of coffee culture denounced the beverage as promoting "immoral behavior." The pressure from critics grew until 1511, when religious officials in Mecca ordered a ban on coffee. But by then it was already too late. The decree was not enforceable beyond the city, and coffee's economic and social benefits far outweighed the wishes of religious authorities in Mecca. Ultimately, this effort and others like it to suppress coffee culture proved futile. As Sufis increasingly introduced the drink to non-Sufis, Mocha merchants too saw the economic potential, added the commodity to their trade networks, and promoted coffee to a variety of customers. What had first emerged in critical mass in Mocha and Mecca in time became a regular feature across the Muslim world.[8]

---

7. Ralph Hattox, *Coffee and Coffeehouses: The Origins of a Social Beverage in the Medieval Near East* (Seattle: University of Washington Press, 1985), 14.

8. Catherine M. Tucker, *Coffee Culture: Local Experiences, Global Connections* (London: Routledge, 2011), 51–52.

In the early sixteenth century, Yemeni Sufis studying at al-Azhar University brought coffee to the city of Cairo, then located in the Mamluk Sultanate (modern-day Egypt), but its demand remained minor until the Ottomans conquered Yemen in the 1530s. Their military victory linked trade networks across the Red Sea to Cairo. Authorities in the Ottoman Empire fully realized the economic value of coffee. In 1534 opponents of Sufism, led by a local religious leader named Abd al-Hakk al-Sunbati, denounced coffee. They even destroyed several Cairo coffee-houses due to their association with Sufism. Al-Sunbati's supporters wanted coffee banned in the city, but during the hearing the chief judge tried the beverage and sided with the coffee drinkers.[9] Why was the judge swayed? One answer might be that he just loved the taste of the drink, but a more likely interpretation is that coffee was part of the growing Ottoman trade network, and the judge grasped its economic value. As we can see the spread of coffee was not inevitable, but linked to religious, political, and economic choices by those involved in the trade. Merchants introduced coffee across Ottoman areas quickly. Two Syrian merchants, Halim and Shams, introduced coffee to Istanbul (the Ottoman capital) in 1554; twelve years later, there were over six hundred coffeehouses in the city.[10]

Coffee continued to grow in favor across the Ottoman Empire. By 1538 Yemen became an outlying political province within the Ottoman Empire, but it remained the central location for coffee production and a key hub of economic activity on the Arabian Peninsula. Producers grew the coffee in the area near Mocha, and merchants roasted and ground the beans in the major cities for shipment. While the city of Hudaydah served as the main shipment center for coffee across the Ottoman Empire, Mocha retained its status as the central port for coffee's distribution beyond the Ottoman realm and into the wider Indian Ocean economy (See Map 1.1). Historian Nancy Um convincingly argues that Mocha's rise as a global port can be attributed to the arrival of the Ottomans during the early sixteenth century.[11] By the late fifteenth century the Ottomans had already expanded down the Red Sea coast, in part as a response to increased Portuguese commercial and naval activities in the western Indian Ocean. Ottoman rulers hoped to profit from the lucrative Indian Ocean trade and to thwart potential Portuguese rivals, so they began to support the Bayans, the north Indian immigrant family that had already begun to build viable economic networks across the Indian Ocean by the time the Ottomans reached Yemen.

As the Bayans scaled up their coffee enterprise in Mocha, other commodities followed. Spices from India and Southeast Asia, Chinese silks and textiles

---

9. Hattox, *Coffee and Coffeehouses*, 27.

10. Antony Wild, *Coffee: A Dark History* (London: Harper Collins, 2004), 53.

11. Nancy Um, *The Merchant Houses of Mocha* (Seattle: University of Washington Press, 2003), 21.

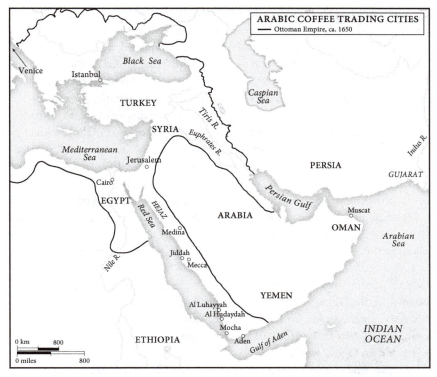

MAP 1.1 Arabic Coffee-Trading Cities

from India, and bulk metals from East and Southeast Asia (tin, copper, steel, lead, and iron) all made their way through the port. Merchants traded porcelains from Asia (including small coffee cups) and powdered sugar, dyestuffs, rice, oil, and ghee (purified butter) from India. Ships leaving Mocha carried bullion and coins to the Indian coast. Even Europeans, only minor actors in the Ottoman-dominated Indian Ocean economy in the early sixteenth century, carried coffee back to Europe. So too did the regional coffee trade within the Ottoman Empire expand. By the seventeenth century, for example, the economy of coffee imports and exports constituted one-third of Egypt's foreign commerce.[12] In short, coffee had become big business by the sixteenth century, both regionally and globally.[13] While some Yemenis sought to maintain the near monopoly on planting, others established coffee farms in India and Ceylon (today, Sri Lanka).[14] This early

12. Um, *The Merchant Houses of Mocha*, 44.

13. Hattox, *Coffee and Coffeehouses*, 72.

14. Gregory Dicum and Nina Luttinger, *The Coffee Book: Anatomy of an Industry from Crop to the Last Drop* (New York: The New Press, 1999), 6.

example of outsourcing allowed merchants to cut down on transportation costs. As growers plunged coffee plants into the soil in South Asia, a period of market expansion and wealth accumulation developed amidst ideal political stability at both ends of the Indian Ocean system—from Ming China in the east to the Ottoman Empire in the west. It was in this political and economic context that European merchants found themselves by the early seventeenth century.

As the coffee market expanded, European merchants saw opportunities for profit. Europeans first encountered coffee in Cairo at the outset of the seventeenth century. Yemeni producers sold the roasted coffee to other merchants while keeping a monopoly on the plants. By the 1620s the British East India Company purchased coffee from Arab merchants, and actively traded coffee from Yemen across the Arabian Sea to the Indian and Asian market.[15] Dutch merchants started bringing it back to Amsterdam for the European market from the Indian Ocean as well. Business boomed for nearly all merchants in the coffee game. The boom of the Yemeni coffee market lasted until the 1680s, when internal turmoil in China and wars in Europe limited the demand for exports.[16] Also, the Japanese markets, while only a small portion of the trade, closed due to the isolationist policies of the Tokugawa government. Europe's markets rebounded by 1700, but Asian markets were slower to recover. More importantly, however, dramatic changes elsewhere shifted the balance of economic and eventually political power in the Indian Ocean world.

At the time of the Yemeni coffee collapse of the 1680s, Europeans had accumulated large sums of capital from their colonial ventures in the Americas for the better part of 150 years. Once minor players in the Indian Ocean, European trading companies began to use the wealth amassed through gold and silver mining and through plantation slavery to dictate the terms of trade in the Indian Ocean. By the early eighteenth century, European merchants could move coffee faster and in greater quantities than their local counterparts. Moreover, European merchants secured coffee trees and planted them outside of Ethiopia and Yemen after 1699, which allowed them to undercut Arab domination of the coffee trade. European merchants now produced and sold the majority of the coffee in the Indian Ocean region at the same time that they profited from their American colonies. These twinned enterprises resulted in the emergence of a truly global coffee trade at the precise moment that control of that trade slipped from the grasp of the Bayans and other Yemen-based coffee merchants. But like the advent of coffee culture itself, this transition in power was neither inevitable nor uncontested.

---

15. Wild, *Coffee*, 69.

16. Anthony Reid, *Southeast Asia in the Age of Commerce, 1450–1680: Volume 2, Expansion and Crisis* (New Haven, CT: Yale University Press, 1995), 285.

In 1658 European merchants tried breaking the Ottoman coffee monopoly, but most attempts were unsuccessful. In 1699, Dutch merchants succeeded when they stole coffee plants from Yemen and planted them in Java.[17] Within twenty years, the Dutch East Indies (present-day Indonesia) was the world's leading coffee producer. As European merchant colonies spread through the area, coffee production for export spread as well. Other European powers quickly obtained coffee seedlings in order to enter the growing coffee trade. The main exporters during the eighteenth century were the Dutch on Java and Sumatra, the French on the tiny island of Réunion (near Madagascar), and the British on Ceylon. Réunion was a major producer for only a short period in the 1710s, and French operations ended by the 1750s due to British pressure, plant fungus, and the collapse of the French East India Company.[18] French coffee production was then moved to new fields in Madagascar. In India, coffee production had flourished under the control of Muslim merchants, but as Great Britain moved into India they took over the Indian coffee trade. The British expanded their colonial presence in India in the eighteenth century until they dominated the subcontinent both economically and politically. The expansion of the imperial presence of Great Britain will be examined in more detail in chapter 3.

In order to understand the growing domination of European merchants in the Indian Ocean trade, we will examine the growing spread of coffee in Europe. Until the seventeenth century coffee was a curiosity to most Europeans. This changed around the middle of the seventeenth century when a whole set of little-known exotic commodities became fashionable. Chocolate, tobacco, and coffee made a grand entrance into European luxury culture.[19] The introduction of coffee and coffee culture to Europe drove the European interest in the Indian Ocean coffee trade, leading to proto-globalization. Venetian merchants came in contact with Yemen coffee in the early seventeenth century in Istanbul and brought it back with them. However, despite the acclaim of coffee in the Ottoman Empire, at first it was slow to catch on in Europe. Merchants sold coffee in small quantities for medicinal purposes, as European medical authorities believed that coffee sharpened the mind and aided digestion. Merchants imported larger quantities of coffee, promoting the benefits of the beverage increasing use

17. Jonathan Morris, "Coffee: A Condensed History," in *Coffee: A Comprehensive Guide to the Bean, the Beverage, and the Industry*, ed. Robert W. Thurston, Jonathan Morris, and Shawn Steiman (London: Rowman & Littlefield, 2013), 218.

18. Gwyn Campbell, "The Origins and Development of Coffee Production in Réunion and Madagascar, 1711–1972," in *The Global Coffee Economy in Africa, Asia, and Latin America*, ed. William Gervase Clarence-Smith and Steven Topik (Cambridge: Cambridge University Press, 2003), 67–68.

19. Wolfgang Schivelbusch, *Taste of Paradise: A Social History of Spices, Stimulants, and Intoxicants* (New York: Pantheon Books, 1992), 17.

in the Italian states. At first, due to a limited supply the beverage was sold on the street by lemonade vendors, but in 1645 the first coffeehouse opened in Italy as the supply increased.[20]

In the major cities of England, France, Holland, and the Holy Roman Empire, coffeehouses quickly become centers of social activity and communication due to the stimulating effects of the drug, which increased the demand for it from the Indian Ocean region (See Figure 1.1). European merchants increased their involvement in the Indian Ocean coffee trade as demand grew. In 1637 merchants introduced Turkish coffee (from Mocha) at Oxford, where students and professors established the Oxford Coffee Club.[21] Coffeehouses appeared in London in 1652, and by 1660 they were an integral part of its social and political culture. The general public dubbed coffeehouses "Penny Universities," as they were patronized by writers, artists, poets, lawyers, politicians and philosophers.[22] The entrance fee of one penny allowed coffee drinkers access to intellectual conversations and debate.

FIGURE 1.1 Interior of London Coffeehouse c. 1690–1700. The image demonstrates the community atmosphere of the early coffeehouses.
Source: British Museum image - © The Trustees of the British Museum.

---

20. Mark Pendergrast, *Uncommon Grounds: The History of Coffee and How It Transformed Our World* (New York: Basic Books, 2010), 8.

21. Alan Bennet Weinberg and Bonnie K. Bealer, *The World of Caffeine: The Science and Culture of the World's Most Popular Drug* (Abingdon, UK: Routledge, 2002), 151.

22. Weinberg and Bealer, *The World of Caffeine,* 154.

What caused the esteem of coffee with a wide segment of the English population? Coffee stimulated conversation and social contact but did not dull the senses like alcohol, echoing the attraction in Arab areas. The concept was that coffee provided a long list of medical benefits, but a major factor was that coffee was a sober beverage. The late seventeenth-century middle classes regarded coffee as the great soberer, leaving individuals sharp of mind and efficient at business.[23] Coffee drinking increased and by the mid-seventeenth century, there were over three hundred coffeehouses in London. Coffee drinking was a central part of business in England as well. Lloyd's of London began in Lloyd's Coffee House, opened by Edward Lloyd in 1686 on Tower Street.[24] The coffeehouse was frequented by sailors, merchants, and ship owners, and Lloyd provided them reliable shipping news. The establishment soon became recognized as the best place to purchase marine insurance. The coffeehouse was also a favorite spot for slave traders, and Lloyd's insured slaves and slave ships as well.[25] Lloyd's obtained a monopoly on maritime insurance related to the slave trade and maintained it until the early nineteenth century.

The English crown saw the rise of coffeehouses across London as a threat, similar to the way local Arab authorities viewed them. On December 23, 1675, King Charles II of England issued "A Proclamation for the Suppression of Coffee Houses" in the *London Gazette*. The proclamation stated:

> Whereas it is most apparent that the multitude of Coffee Houses of late years set up and kept within this Kingdom . . . and the great resort of idle and disaffected persons to them, have produced very much of their time, which might and probably would be employed in and about their Lawful Calling and Affairs; but also for that in such houses . . . divers, false, malitious, and scandalous reports are devised and spread abroad to the Defamation of His Majesty's Government, and to the disturbance of the Peace and Quiet of the Realm; his Majesty hath thought it fit and necessary, that the said Coffee Houses be (for the Future) put down and suppressed.[26]

---

23. Schivelbusch, *Taste of Paradise*, 19.

24. Lloyd's of London is an insurance market that allows groups of financial backers to come together to pool and spread the risk in insurance policies. See also G. J. Marcus, *Heart of Oak: A Survey of British Sea Power in the Georgian Era* (New York: Oxford University Press, 1975), 192.

25. Eric Williams, *Capitalism & Slavery* (Richmond, VA: The William Byrd Press, 1944), 104–05.

26. E. A. Drew, "Clubland Two Hundred Years Ago," *The Living Age* Issue 280 (Mar. 21, 1914): 733.

As we can see from this proclamation, Charles II found the growing coffee culture dangerous. The king believed that large groups of men gathering and criticizing his rule undermined his government. Political authorities made a choice to ban coffee due to the political ramifications of coffee *culture*, not the drug itself. Charles revoked the ban on January 8, 1676, due to widespread citizen protest, which threatened the crown even more.

Coffee entered the Holy Roman Empire (Germany, Austria, and other regions of central Europe) in 1683 with the end of the Second Siege of Vienna. The Ottoman Empire and Holy Roman Empire clashed on several occasions over the previous one hundred years, and the siege of Vienna was a major battle in this ongoing conflict. When the armies of the Ottoman Turks retreated they were forced to abandon their supplies, which included large amounts of coffee.[27] The armies of the Holy Roman Empire failed to identify the sacks of beans, but an Austrian spy named Kolschitzky recognized them. Kolschitzky had spent a large amount of time in the Ottoman Empire due to his occupation, and while there he developed a taste for coffee. He was able to claim the bags of coffee beans and decided to go into business. Kolschitzky served small cups of Turkish coffee to the Viennese, first going door to door, and then establishing a coffeehouse in a large tent. Kolschitzky made an economic prediction that coffee drinking would be fashionable with consumers. Coffee drinking spread, but coffeehouses developed slowly as the coffee supply entered the German states almost exclusively through the Ottoman supply chain by way of Italy. Due to conflict between the Holy Roman Empire and the Ottoman Empire, supply was limited. This changed by the mid-eighteenth century when Atlantic merchants started to dominate the trade through France and England to Hamburg.[28]

The growing demand for coffee in Europe convinced merchants of the value of the commodity, leading to them to dominate the Indian Ocean coffee trade. The coffee trade was not inevitable, but resulted from merchants making deliberate economic decisions to control and increase production to turn a profit. This was at times in opposition to political and religious authorities who saw the drink and the practices surrounding it a threat. European merchants moved production to new colonies in the Atlantic World, fully globalizing the market in the eighteenth century. We can see that the spread of coffee was contingent on the choices and actions of not only consumers but producers, merchants, and religious and political authorities. Globalization was not a mechanical process; it was a complex juxtaposition of all of these groups.

---

27. Bob Biderman, *A People's History of Coffee and Cafes* (Cambridge: Black Apollo Press, 2013), 100.

28. Biderman, *A People's History of Coffee and Cafes*, 101.

Tobacco: An Atlantic Ocean History

When Christopher Columbus arrived in the Bahamas on October 15, 1492, the natives gave him a gift of dried tobacco leaves. He documented the encounter in his journal.

> He had a little of their bread, about the size of a fist, a calabash of water, a piece of brown earth [pigment] powdered and then kneaded, and some dried leaves, which must be a thing highly valued by them, for they bartered with it at San Salvador.[29]

Initially Columbus was interested in the dried tobacco leaves only because the natives found them valuable, but after he tried tobacco decided it may have economic potential in Spain. Tobacco is another component of proto-globalization, as European merchants developed an Atlantic Ocean trade in the sixteenth century that would lead to the drug spreading across the world.

After Columbus introduced tobacco to the political elite, they adopted the new drug as an exotic medicine and as a sign of social status. What made this new drug so popular? At first medical authorities considered the drug medicinally useful, and users focused primarily on its mild calming effect. As early as 1525, several Spanish medical authorities described the smoking of tobacco as "clarifying the mind and providing happy thoughts."[30] As we can see by this statement, some physicians perceived tobacco as having a calming effect on the senses without totally incapacitating the consumer. At this time Europeans credited exotic realms, such as the Americas, with miraculous medicines.[31] Doctors also used tobacco to lessen the pain of earaches and toothaches, but the calming aspect of the drug was the main draw. While coffee cleared and stimulated the mind, tobacco calmed the overexcited mind, leading to better decisions.[32] The demand of the drug combined perceived health benefits, the social status of the drug, and its addictive qualities. By the 1570s, tobacco entered into regular consumption patterns in Europe.[33] However, not all European political authorities universally

---

29. Christopher Columbus, *The Journal of Christopher Columbus* (Madison: Wisconsin Historical Society, 2003), 117.

30. Vertress J. Wyckoff, *Tobacco Regulation in Colonial Maryland* (Baltimore: John Hopkins University Press, 1936), 51.

31. Marcy Norton, *Sacred Gifts, Profane Pleasures: A History of Tobacco and Chocolate in the Atlantic World* (Ithaca, NY: Cornell University Press, 2008), 143.

32. Schivelbusch, *Tastes of Paradise*, 107.

33. Jordan Goodman. *Tobacco in History: The Culture of Dependence* (London: Routledge, 1993), 59.

accepted the drug. Many found the breathing in of smoke to be odd and possibly dangerous, while others did not like being exposed to smoke created by users. What caused these authorities to question the medical perception? A likely interpretation is that access to tobacco was improving the economic and political status of some individuals, which threatened the economic position of others.

After the Spanish introduced tobacco to Europeans around 1528, the demand for the drug increased among consumers. While addiction played a role, consumers considering the drug an exotic medicine and status symbol played a larger role. By 1558 Jesuit monks were growing it at their mission for export to Spain.[34] The Spanish and Portuguese rolled the dried leaves into cigars, and Jean Nicot, French ambassador in Lisbon, sent some to Paris in 1559 after trying them. The word "nicotine" derives from Jean Nicot's cigars. The French, Spanish, and Portuguese initially stressed the medicinal properties of the plant, and in 1571 a Spanish doctor, Nicolas Monardes, stated that tobacco could cure thirty-six health problems.[35] Spanish merchants introduced tobacco into England, but Sir Walter Raleigh, who was held in esteem, made the drug fashionable. Raleigh returned to England from the Americas in 1586, with colonists from the settlement on Roanoke Island bringing tobacco, as well as maize and potatoes. Raleigh hoped Roanoke would be economically successful; he thought that increasing the fame of tobacco would aid him in this endeavor. He heavily promoted the new drug as a necessary recreation for all gentlemen (the lowest rank of English gentry). He smoked constantly, and soon other elites saw smoking as the height of fashion. Men's clubs and hunting parties started consuming tobacco by smoking pipes.

Tobacco spread to other locations due to European trade influences, but consumers continued to enjoy the drug for a perceived medical benefit and calming effect. As European explorers and merchants traveled around the world, they brought tobacco with them. The Spanish introduced it to the Philippines from Mexico in 1575 as part of their maritime trade.[36] The Spanish quickly established it as a cash crop in the islands. Chinese sailors encountered it in the Philippines and carried it back to China at the turn of the seventeenth century. The Portuguese spread the use of the plant across Southeast Asia from their merchant base in Macao; they introduced it to India around 1575, Java in 1600, and into Japan by 1605. Due to its perceived medicinal effects, tobacco moved along the established trade networks that were connecting regions around the world as part of proto-globalization.

Japanese merchants carried it to Korea, and it traveled along Chinese trade routes into Siberia, Mongolia, and Tibet. By the 1630s local farmers cultivated

---

34. V. G. Kiernan, *Tobacco: A History* (London: Hutchinson Radius, 1991), 12.

35. Norton, *Sacred Gifts, Profane Pleasures*, 107.

36. Goodman, *Tobacco in History*, 51.

it in various locations in present-day Indochina and Formosa. In the early seventeenth century the Portuguese introduced tobacco to Persia, and the British into the Ottoman Empire. By 1630 a variety of European merchants sold it in West Africa, and it was sold in East Africa by Portuguese and Arabic merchants. Merchants started to cultivate it globally and diverse cultures adopted it for its perceived medical benefits. Of course, the calming and addictive properties of the drug helped, but the efforts of merchants and limited opposition from political and religious authorities in the early seventeenth century increased its availability. However, production could not keep up with demand. This changed when a small Atlantic colony perfected new method of raising and curing tobacco in large quantities.

Merchants needing more sources of production turned to colonies in the New World. A group of English entrepreneurs received a charter from the Virginia Company of London (also known as the London Company) to establish a colony in the New World for this very purpose. The London Company founded Jamestown in the Chesapeake Bay region in 1607. After a few very hard years in which many colonists died, Jamestown colonists began growing tobacco for the English market, but English consumers disliked native tobacco from Virginia as they preferred the flavor of sweeter Spanish varieties. This changed after John Rolfe arrived in the new colony in 1610. Rolfe introduced sweeter strains of tobacco from Trinidad, using Spanish seeds he brought with him. In 1612 he started to export the new strains, grown with new techniques that he had developed by studying various cultivators in the New World. As we will see, Rolfe turned the Virginia Colony into a profitable venture using his global knowledge of the drug. Rolfe named his Virginia-grown strain of the tobacco Orinoco, a variety that appealed to consumers due to its high nicotine content and sweeter flavor. Rolfe and others soon exported vast quantities of the new cash crop. This led to an expansion in tobacco cultivation; producers established new plantations along the James River, and cultivation moved inland.

Tobacco had a profound impact on the transatlantic North American economy. In 1616–1617, Virginia exported 2,300 pounds to London, compared to the 58,300 pounds Spain exported.[37] Within two years, the Virginia Colony shipped more than 20,000 pounds, and in 1620 the colony exported 40,000 pounds to England. As the tobacco trade increased, colonists made allies in the political and mercantile sectors in England. Tobacco became a major part of the economy, and tobacco merchants increased their political and social influence and thwarted any critics of tobacco. In 1620, colonists used tobacco as legal tender in the colonies of Maryland and Virginia, demonstrating its central role in North American colonies.

---

37. Norton, *Sacred Gifts, Profane Pleasures*, 162.

Tobacco farming and curing is labor intensive, so producers needed a source of cheap labor. Sugar producers had already established slave markets, so slavery quickly expanded to tobacco. While all tobacco plantations in the Atlantic World turned to African slavery as they expanded their operations after the 1680s, we will focus on the colonies in Virginia and Maryland to highlight the shift from free indentured servants to slave labor, since these colonies dominated the tobacco market. At first tobacco farms used poor English immigrants, indentured for a fixed period of time, in return for their fare to the New World. This provided a quick labor source, as large numbers Londoners needed employment due to poor economic conditions in England. This changed in the late seventeenth century for several reasons. Producers found indentured servants a detriment in the long run, as the majority of servants, after being released from their debt, turned to tobacco farming themselves. Plantation owners realized that they trained their future competition. By the 1680s rising wages in England shrank the pool of unemployed workers, which limited the number of indentured servants. Sugar plantations used African slavery in the Caribbean, so slave merchants transitioned to tobacco farms. Slavery first became legal in Virginia and Maryland in 1660, but indentured servants outnumbered slaves. A major shift happened when the Royal African Company lost their monopoly on carrying slaves to the colonies.[38] What impact did this loss of monopoly have on the slave trade? Any merchant or trading company now could ship slaves to the North American colonies. The number of slaves in the colonies dramatically increased. From 1700 to1750 tens of thousands of slaves arrive in America, and by the end of the seventeenth century over one million slaves had been shipped to the Chesapeake Bay region, with most of the increase being due to the expansion of tobacco plantations.[39] Slaves served as the backbone of the tobacco economy. The increased production was not possible without them, and we can see that slavery was closely intertwined with success of the drug's production.

As the demand for tobacco grew in the early seventeenth century, non-English producers cultivated more land to compete. Spain increased production in Mexico, Trinidad, Cuba, Puerto Rico, Santo Domingo, Honduras, and Venezuela, while Portugal developed tobacco plantations across northern Brazil. The Portuguese had introduced tobacco to India, and Indian merchants grew it for export to Mocha and the Arabian market, but it could not compete with the Atlantic market as Indian tobacco was considered weak, and mostly used locally.[40]

---

38. The Royal African company was a partnership of the royal Stuart family and London merchants. After the Glorious Revolution in England, royal power weakened, and the company lost power.

39. Allan Kulikoff, *Tobacco and Slaves: The Development of Southern Cultures in the Chesapeake, 1680–1800* (Chapel Hill: University of North Carolina Press, 1986), 80.

40. B. G. Gokhale. "Tobacco in Seventeenth-Century India," *Agricultural History* 48, no. 4 (October 1974): 485.

The main producer continued to be the Chesapeake colonies. By 1700 Spain and Portugal exported over five million pounds per year, but the Chesapeake exported forty million pounds annually.[41] London dominated the tobacco trade, with 80 percent of the drug moving through the markets of the city. Merchants then shipped tobacco across Europe, the coast of Africa, and into Asia. By the mid-seventeenth century, prices dropped increasing consumption to a degree— though prices fell faster than per capita consumption rose.

Smokers commonly consumed tobacco using pipes, and no prohibition on age or gender existed in the seventeenth century (See Figure 1.2). Smoking and drinking alcohol went hand in hand, as taverns across Europe sold tobacco alongside liquor. The practice of using snuff (inhaled powdered tobacco) grew in the seventeenth century as well. The Portuguese introduced the practice after observing its use by the indigenous population of Brazil. The Dutch, who named the ground, powdered tobacco "snuff," used the product by 1560 as an expensive luxury commodity. This changed in the mid-seventeenth century as snuff use moved across Europe, Asia, and Africa. Snuff merchants made the product available to all ages, and in order to increase sales added a variety of spice, fruit, and floral flavors using unique recipes and blends, as well as special recipes for individual customers.[42] Common flavors included coffee, chocolate, honey, vanilla,

FIGURE 1.2 The earliest image of a man smoking a pipe, which was the common way to consume tobacco globally.
Source: Walter Raleigh - ©iStock/powerofforever

41. Goodman, *Tobacco in History*, 64.

42. George Evans and Friboug & Treyer, *The Old Snuff House of Fribourg & Treyer at the Sign of the Rasp & Crown, No.34 St. James's Haymarket, London, S.W.* (London: Nabu Press, 1720, 1920), 15.

cherry, orange, plum, apricot, camphor, rose, and spearmint. This made the drug desired in all segments of society.

Coffee started as an Indian Ocean trade item in the fifteenth century, and tobacco began as an Atlantic Ocean commodity in the sixteenth century. As we move into the seventeenth century, merchants established both of these drugs as global trade items. The trade in rum, the third drug we will examine in this chapter, began slightly differently. Rum traveled along these fully established trade routes not as a commodity but mainly due to its use by naval personnel, who introduced this little-known beverage along these established trade routes and thus created a demand, thereby turning it into a global commodity.

Rum: Global Maritime Trade

According to legend, sailors preserved Vice Admiral Horatio Nelson of the British Royal Navy, following his victory and death at the Battle of Trafalgar (1805), in a cask of rum for transport. Upon arrival in England, naval officials opened the cask and found it empty. Nelson's thirsty men drilled a hole in the bottom of the cask and drank the rum, originating the term "Nelson's blood" to describe rum.[43] What can this nineteenth-century legend tell us about the seventeenth century and proto-globalization? European navies introduced rum to various parts of the world during their travels, which in turn created a demand for the drink. This story illustrates the popularity of rum with the British Royal Navy and by the nineteenth century, it was accepted as fact that naval personnel would do anything to acquire rum. Rum became a useful commodity among merchants, as it used large supplies of sugar and generated more income with less bulk transportation costs. The beverage plays a role in proto-globalization, as European navies introduced the drink along trade routes and merchants took advantage of its renown to increase production.

People produced most alcohol locally until the sixteenth century, when worldwide commerce spread and alcohol became a global commodity. While gin, whiskey, and bourbon were available across large areas, this section will focus on rum, which ws the first to spread globally. Merchants traded coffee and tobacco regionally and then globally as demand for the drugs increased, and political and religious opposition decreased. Rum traveled the globe in a different way. During proto-globalization, as European navies moved around the world transporting goods and establishing merchant colonies, they carried rum with them for their own consumption. As a result they introduced rum to various parts of the world, increasing a desire for the drink. What this means is that merchants increased the

---

43. James Pack, *Nelson's Blood: The Story of Naval Rum* (Annapolis: Naval Institute Press, 1982), 55.

amount of coffee and tobacco sold, making them global commodities due to a demand for the drugs, while merchants only transported rum around the world for the ship's crews, which after being shared created a new interest in rum. In order to understand the growth and production of rum, first we need to discuss sugar and slavery.

The history of Atlantic commerce is inseparable from the history of slavery, and the transfer of both labor and capital across the Atlantic is closely connected with sugar production. The available supply of sugar could not meet the demand in Europe, which led merchants to look for more locations for production. Sugar cultivation in the Americas filled this need, requiring both large investments of capital and a steady supply of labor.[44] Labor was a problem for the new plantations, since many Europeans did not want to relocate to the Caribbean, and disease had a major impact on Native Americans. Europeans turned to African slavery as the solution. As sugar plantations spread throughout the Caribbean and the coast of South America, the number of African slaves grew as well. The reliance of sugar plantations on slavery meant that by the eighteenth century, Africans significantly outnumbered Europeans in the Caribbean region.[45] Sugar and slavery helped link the Americas, Europe, and Africa in a complex trade economy. As sugar started to dominate the landscape, plantations became bigger to produce more for the European demand. As plantations increased in size cheaper labor was needed, increasing the demand for slaves. By 1600 slave traders had shipped around 200,000 Africans to plantations, and fifty years later, the number of slaves increased to 800,000.[46]

On the sugar plantations of the Caribbean, colonists and slaves used sugarcane juice and its byproducts to produce fermented alcoholic drinks.[47] Slaves fermented molasses and sugar waste, and tapped palm trees to make palm wine.[48] Some of these fermented drinks became the prototypes for the distillation of rum. In the early seventeenth century slaves created small stills, leading to the first distillation of rum on the island of Barbados. The English settled Barbados in 1627, trying a variety of cash crops, including cotton, indigo, and tobacco;

44. Candice Goucher, Charles LeGuin, and Linda Walton, *Commerce and Change: The Creation of a Global Economy and the Expansion of Europe* (Boston: McGraw-Hill, 1998), 492.

45. Goucher, LeGuin, and Walton, *Commerce and Change*, 492.

46. P. C. Emmer, "The Dutch and the Making of the Second Atlantic System," in *Slavery and the Rise of the Atlantic System*, ed. Barbara Solow (Cambridge: Cambridge University Press, 1991), 80.

47. Frederick H. Smith, *Caribbean Rum: A Social and Economic History* (Tampa: University Press of Florida, 2005), 10.

48. Anthony Dias Blue, *The Complete Book of Spirits: A Guide to Their History, Production, and Enjoyment* (New York: HarperCollins, 2004), 70.

however, by 1631 the English introduced sugar production. It is not clear when the distillation of rum began on Barbados, but by the late 1630s sugar plantation owners served it in small quantities to guests on the island.[49] Sugar production increased in 1647, and by 1650 it was the main cash crop. As sugar production increased, slavery and the production of rum increased as well.

Caribbean and North American Rum

At first consumers drank rum in the local Caribbean market, as access to other spirits was limited. Local merchants did not consider rum a major commodity, but rather a longer-lasting substitute for beer, as sailors wanted alcohol for long maritime voyages. The belief that distilled alcohol provided medicinal benefits helped spread its use. As rum manufacturing increased on Barbados, Dutch merchants, who regularly purchased sugar from the English island, started to ship rum around the Caribbean. The Dutch also traded for sugar with the French on Martinique. Why did Dutch merchants decide to start trafficking in rum? The Dutch made a deliberate economic decision, as shipping casks of rum was easier than shipping the bulkier sugar. They could also charge a higher price for rum than for the same amount of sugar. However, most consumers knew little about rum, so merchants needed to increase its appeal to sell their product.

In 1644 Benjamin Da Costa, a Dutch Jew from Brazil, introduced the equipment to Martinique to start producing rum.[50] We can see the impact of early globalization in this example, as people of different nationalities and religions, as well as commodities, were moving around the world. At this point rum distillation moved through the French and English holdings in the Caribbean. The value of rum was clearly apparent to European merchants; one gallon of rum was equal in value to ten pounds of sugar. In the early seventeenth century most of the rum produced was consumed in the islands, but as merchants intentionally introduced rum into other areas, exports increased. In 1666, plantations on Barbados were exporting 150,000 gallons outside the region.[51] Large plantations produced most of the rum in the Caribbean using slave labor to process the beverage, highlighting that large-scale drug production was closely intertwined with the Atlantic slave trade. Barbados continued to be the main Caribbean rum producer until 1680, when Jamaica took the lead. But as consumption increased, the production moved out of the islands.

After Europeans established rum production in the Caribbean, production eventually moved to Colonial North America. The North American colonies acquired the majority of rum from Barbados, but the demand outpaced the supply.

---

49. Smith, *Caribbean Rum*, 15.

50. Smith, *Caribbean Rum*, 14.

51. Smith, *Caribbean Rum*, 23.

To support the growing demand and to save on transportation costs, a group of producers in 1664 established a new distillery on present-day Staten Island. Three years later businessmen established another distillery in Boston.[52] The manufacture of rum was one of early Colonial New England's largest and most prosperous industries, and Boston merchants preferred to barter with rum as it was easier to ship and could be stored for long periods of time. It is important for us to understand that converting sugar into rum saved on transportation costs and allowed for longer storage periods, which made rum a lucrative product. The 110,000 residents in the British North American colonies consumed per capita three gallons of rum per year.[53] In the seventeenth century, North American fur traders used Caribbean rum as a major part of their business, bringing Native Americans into the drug's trade network. French and English fur traders used rum to barter for furs, seal agreements with native groups, and as gifts to ease trade. Rum moved across North America on these new trading networks. Merchants sold rum across the Spanish-American colonies, as the price of Spanish wine and brandy was too high for many consumers due to high import taxes. Spanish colonies in central and South America attempted to produce rum, but these ventures could not compete with the rum from British and French holdings in the Caribbean.

As the European navies moved around the world, they carried rum with them. The main naval use of rum started in 1655 when the British Royal Navy captured Jamaica. With rum being produced in Barbados and Jamaica, the British Navy had access to large amounts of domestically produced rum.[54] The British changed the daily ration of liquor given to seamen from French brandy (distilled wine) to rum, which saved them the cost of importing the brandy. As the British navy traveled around the world, rum went with them. Other navies imitated the British Royal Navy's rum ration, but none continued with it for as long. For example, the United States navy started issuing a rum ration in 1794 but replaced it with whiskey (distilled grain) by 1806. The Royal Navy continued to give its sailors a daily rum ration, known as a "tot," until July 31, 1970. European navies introduced rum into many regions of the world as they traveled the globe. This introduction created a demand, thereby increasing the rum trade.

The Eighteenth Century: A Global Trade in Drugs

By the eighteenth century the sale and production of coffee, tobacco, and rum was global as merchants produced and sold these drugs across North and South America, Europe, Africa, and Asia. European merchants dominating coffee

---

52. Smith, *Caribbean Rum*, 31.

53. Reay Tannahill, *Food in History* (New York: Stein and Day, 1973), 295.

54. Pack, *Nelson's Blood*, 14.

production moved to the Atlantic World in the early eighteenth century. Gabriel de Clieu, a French naval officer, introduced coffee plants to Martinique in the Caribbean in 1720. The plants flourished and within fifty years the island was home to over 18,680 coffee trees.[55] The success in Martinique led to cultivation on Saint-Domingue (Haiti), Mexico, and other islands of the Caribbean. French colonial plantations on Martinique and Saint-Domingue used slave labor for sugar production, and quickly moved the labor to coffee plantations. The French, English, and Dutch established coffee slave plantations on Jamaica, St. Vincent, Grenada, St. Lucia, Trinidad, and Demerara.

Coffee production would also play a role in the first successful slave revolt that created an independent country. Slave conditions on Saint-Domingue plantations were horrendous, with 500,000 slaves producing sugar and coffee.[56] Due to the deplorable treatment by the owners, the Haitian Revolution started when slaves rebelled in 1791, driving the French owners off the island and earning their freedom. The former slaves—the majority from coffee plantations—then helped form the new state of Haiti. After the slave revolt, the coffee industry on Haiti never fully recovered.[57]

In the British colonies in North America, tea continued to be the favored drink until 1773. Coffee cost more, and colonists viewed it as a European and therefore elitist drink. Colonists considered tea their everyday drink. This changed with the passage of the Tea Act of 1773. The British government attempted to reduce the surplus of tea held by British East India Company to help the struggling company survive.[58] The British government wanted to undercut the price of illegal tea and limit its smuggling into colonies as well. The act forced colonists to buy only East India Company tea, which led the Sons of Liberty to stage the Boston Tea Party revolt on December 16, 1773, where they destroyed an entire shipment of tea.[59] At this point a major shift occurred and colonists switched from tea to coffee.[60] Before this time the wealthier classes consumed coffee, while the less prosperous consumed tea. Colonists now saw tea as British and elitist, and coffee as American and common.

---

55. Stewart Lee Allen, *The Devil's Cup: A History of the World According to Coffee* (New York: Ballantine Books, 1999), 170.

56. Possible student research topic: slave conditions on coffee plantations and the relationship to the Haitian Revolution. Jeremy D. Popkins, *A Concise History of the Haitian Revolution* (Malden: Wiley-Blackwell, 2012) and David Patricj Geggus, *The Impact of the Haitian Revolution on the Atlantic World* (Colombia: University of South Carolina Press, 2001).

57. Pendergrast, *Uncommon Grounds*, 16.

58. Chapter 2 will discuss the East India Company, tea, and the opium trade.

59. This was not the only East India Tea destroyed, as shipments were destroyed in several colonial port cities.

60. Wild, *Coffee*, 130–31.

To colonists, drinking coffee expressed freedom, and coffee consumption dramatically increased in the early United States. John Adams, in a letter to his wife Abigail Adams, highlights this change.

> I believe I forgot to tell you one Anecdote: When I first came to this House it was late in the Afternoon, and I had ridden 35 miles at least. "Madam" said I to Mrs. Huston, "is it lawfull for a weary Traveller to refresh himself with a Dish of Tea provided it has been honestly smuggled, or paid no Duties?"
>
> "No sir, said she, we have renounced all Tea in this Place. I cant make Tea, but I'le make you Coffee. Accordingly I have drank Coffee every Afternoon since, and have borne it very well. Tea must be universally renounced. I must be weaned, and the sooner, the better."[61]

As we can see by this quote, American revolutionaries no longer saw tea as American, and coffee drinking dominated the new country. They considered coffee the main beverage of an independent America.

Europeans continued to transform the Indian Ocean coffee trade and production. Arab merchants had first cultivated coffee in Ceylon and traded with the Dutch. The Dutch initially limited their colonialism to maritime trade, and they had a light presence on land until the late seventeenth century. In 1725 the Dutch taxed coffee from villagers in West Java, exporting 1,200 tons a year to Amsterdam.[62] In 1792 the British started to systematically establish coffee farms in India while in the Philippines the Spanish introduced coffee in 1740, and coffee growing spread to various parts of the islands. By the end of the eighteenth century, coffee was a fully globalized commodity.

By the eighteenth century tobacco was a global commodity. European merchants dominated the market, and they shipped New World tobacco around the globe. Trade moved across the Atlantic to Africa, across the Middle East and into India. In Africa tobacco replaced Indian hemp (cannabis), with consumers soon regarding it as second-best compared to tobacco. Merchants sold tobacco across Europe into Russia and Siberia. The Russian government had a mixed relationship with tobacco as at times it was seen as a threat, but the government's view mirrored those of other nations. This changed in 1697 when Peter I (the Great)

---

61. John Adams, "John Adams to Abigail Adams," in *The Adams Papers: Digital Editions: Adams Family Correspondence, Volume 1* (Boston: Massachusetts Historical Society, 6 July 1774), https://www.masshist.org/publications/adams-papers/index.php/volume/ADMS-04-01 Accessed July 3, 2020.

62. Robert McStocker, "The Indonesian Coffee Industry," *Bulletin of Indonesian Economic Studies* 23, no. 1 (1987): 42.

fully legalized the drug. The Russian government attempted to create domestic production, but it was never very successful. Most of the tobacco production and commerce was controlled by other European merchants, with the British being the dominant force. As British colonialism spread around the globe, tobacco exports increased as well. One exception was China, where small farmers produced most tobacco locally, and they used no slave labor.[63] Chinese users did not like European tobacco in the seventeenth and eighteenth centuries, and the local market thrived. China would control their own tobacco market until late eighteenth century. European merchants had no market in China for the drug, which put them at a disadvantage. This would change in the nineteenth century, which will be examined in chapter 3.

As for rum, after 1755 European consumers started preferring rum over other alcohol, and in order to compete with the British and French distilleries, rum production moved across Europe. Denmark, Prussia, and Austria all started to produce their own rum; however, they used primarily Caribbean sugar supplied through the British or French markets.[64] In the eighteenth century the British navy and British colonialism had introduced rum to the rest of the world. As the English moved into the Indian subcontinent, they produced sugar and rum in the region. By this time, European merchants dominated the global drug trade in coffee, tobacco, and rum. In the eighteenth and nineteenth century proto-globalization evolved into modern globalization, and merchants establish two new drugs in the global market, opium and cocaine.

FURTHER READING

Benedict, Carol. *Golden-Silk Smoke: A History of Tobacco in China, 1550–2010* Berkeley: University of California Press, 2011.

Burns, Eric. *The Smoke of the Gods: A Social History of Tobacco* Philadelphia: Temple University Press, 2006.

Morris, Jonathan. "Coffeehouse Formats through the Centuries: Third Places or Public Spaces?" In *Coffee: A Comprehensive Guide to the Bean, the Beverage, and the Industry*, ed. Robert W. Thurston, Jonathan Morris, and Shawn Steiman, 226–233. London: Rowman & Littlefield, 2013.

Phillips, Rod. *Alcohol: A History* Chapel Hill: University of North Carolina Press, 2014.

Ukers, William H. *All About Coffee* Eastford, CT: Martino Fine Books, 2011.

---

63. Carol Benedict, *Golden-Silk Smoke: A History of Tobacco in China, 1550–2010* (Berkeley: University of California Press, 2011), 34.

64. William Ian, *Rum: A Social and Sociable History of the Real Spirit of 1776* (New York: Nation Books, 2005), 258.

2

THE COMMERCIALIZATION OF OPIUM AND COCAINE

In 1821 Thomas De Quincey, a well-known English author, published *The Confessions of an English Opium-Eater*, which laid bare opium addiction. De Quincey wrote that "the marvelous agency of opium, whether for pleasure or for pain," was the hero of the story.[1] It is not clear when De Quincey first used opium—he may have taken it medicinally in 1797 at the age of seventeen or used it a few years later as a student at the University of Oxford to cure toothache and neuralgia.[2] Whenever he first used opium, it's clear that he took it as a medicine. De Quincey described is first taste:

> In an hour, O heavens! What a revulsion! What a resurrection, from the lowest depths, of the inner spirit! What an apocalypse of the world within me. That my pains had vanished was now a trifle in my eyes; this negative effect was swallowed up ... in the abyss of divine enjoyment thus suddenly revealed. Here was a panacea ... for human woes; here was the secret of happiness.[3]

What can we learn from De Quincey's autobiography? On the surface it is clear that opium's addictive qualities dominated the man's life. The author admitted his addiction, but he stressed that the addiction could be managed. However, because De Quincey first used opium for medical conditions, he acquired it easily since at the time it was massproduced. De Quincey also promoted opium's use as an aid to better dreams and innovative thoughts. Like some other nineteenth-century Europeans, De Quincey found opiates attractive because he believed the drugs made the user more creative. Medical authorities promoted opium as a wonder drug, and artists, writers, and scholars promoted it as a stimulant for creative endeavors. Producers and merchants advanced its use in all these areas in order to stimulate trade and generate profits. Merchants marketed opium and opium products (laudanum,

---

1. Thomas De Quincey, *The Confessions of an English Opium-Eater* (London: Bodley Head, 1821), 3.

2. Martin Booth, *Opium: A History* (New York: St. Martin's Press, 1999), 36.

3. De Quincey, *The Confessions*, 13.

morphine, and heroin) as the cure for every type of problem or condition. All of these promotions helped create an increased demand for the drug.

William Halsted's interaction and addiction with cocaine took place later in the nineteenth century. On the morning of May 5, 1885, in lower Manhattan, a construction worker fell from a building's scaffolding.[4] Ambulances rushed the worker, who suffered from a compound fracture of the leg, to Bellevue Hospital. They delivered him to Bellevue since the noted young doctor William Halsted practiced there; he was an expert in serious bone fractures and had a promising and successful career. Before heading to the emergency room to treat the patient, he went to the hospital pharmacy and injected himself with readily available cocaine. When hospital staff summoned Halsted, lost in a drugged and euphoric state, he walked into the operating room, looked at the bloody patient, turned around, and walked out of the hospital in a daze. The patient later died due to infection, and Halsted's career went into decline.[5] How did a brilliant and upcoming young doctor become a cocaine addict? While the addictive nature of cocaine needs to be considered, this story actually highlights the easy availability of cocaine. Halsted regularly prescribed cocaine to his patients for a variety of ailments. By this time hospitals, pharmacies, and stores stocked mass-produced cocaine, morphine, and heroin. Halsted administered these drugs in his profession on a regular basis. He used cocaine as a stimulant to deal with long hours in stressful conditions. Manufacturers promoted the drug as a way to eliminate fatigue, curb hunger pangs, and sharpen the mind. Industrialization and mass production aided in making cocaine one of the major drugs of choice during the nineteenth century.

Throughout the nineteenth century, globalization spread as a direct result of the Industrial Revolution. Opium and cocaine use changed from medicinal to recreational over this period as well. This change is a direct result of the increased supply and demand, driven by the mass production of the Industrial Revolution. Industrialization allowed for the standardized production of household items including medicines while rapid population growth created a sustained demand for commodities. Prior to the Industrial Revolution, most people made a living off the land with the workforce consisting of landowners, tenant farmers, and landless agricultural laborers. Families in various parts of the world commonly spun yarn, wove cloth, and made their own clothing. Some households also spun and wove excess cloth for market production. At the beginning of the Industrial Revolution, India, China, and areas in Asia and the Middle East produced most of the world's cotton cloth, while Europeans produced wool and linen goods. Industrialization changed this dynamic by moving from hand production

---

4. Howard Merkel, *An Anatomy of Addiction: Sigmund Freud, William Halsted, and the Miracle Drug Cocaine* (New York: Vintage Books, 2000), 4.

5. Merkel, *An Anatomy of Addiction*, 8.

methods to machines. Textile production first used industrial production methods, and dominated the Industrial Revolution in terms of employment, value of output, and capital invested.[6] Other developments included new chemical manufacturing and iron production processes, and the rise of the factory system. The factory system used machinery and division of labor to produce manufactured goods. Use of machinery reduced the required skill level of workers and increased the output per worker.[7] The factory system replaced the putting-out system (cottage industry) where people produced goods for market in their homes. In the factory system we see a reliance on machinery, the centralization of factories, and standardization of interchangeable parts. The factory system also contributed to the growth of urban areas, as large numbers of workers migrated into the cities in search of work in the factories.

Steamships reduced the cost of international transport in the nineteenth century and railroads made inland transportation cheaper, and more nations became involved in international trade. Improvements in transportation and communication allowed manufacturers to supply mass-produced items to markets around the world, increasing interaction between people on a worldwide scale and giving rise to the beginnings of modern globalization. Nineteenth-century imperialism, conducted primarily by Western nations, was linked to and synergistic with the Industrial Revolution and decisively shaped globalization. While industrialization, imperialism, and globalization are closely intertwined, for the purpose of this chapter we will only examine industrialization and the resulting commercialization of opioids and cocaine. We will focus on the role of imperialism in globalization in chapter 3.

What can the industrialization and commercialization of drugs tell us about globalization? We started this chapter with the stories of two men, Thomas De Quincey and William Halsted, both of whom, assisted by the industrialization and commercialization of opium and cocaine, became regular users and addicts. However, addiction is not the main focus of this chapter, but rather the choices manufacturers and merchants made to increase the global trade in these drugs. These two men's stories demonstrate the growth of opium and cocaine use from a local phenomenon to globalized manufactured commerce. Since global markets for coffee, tobacco, and alcohol already existed, merchants easily followed the established trade routes with opium and cocaine. By examining the choices made by those involved, we can gain a better understanding of globalization and how these drugs spread around the world. We also need to examine how supply and

---

6. Jeff Horn, Leonard Rosenband, and Merritt Smith, *Reconceptualizing the Industrial Revolution* (Cambridge, MA: MIT Press, 2010), 27.

7. William Walker, "National Innovation Systems: Britain," in *National Innovation Systems: A Comparative Analysis,* ed. Richard Nelson (New York: Oxford University Press, 1993), 187–88.

demand worked together to help create this global market. We will start this examination with the transformation of opium and cocaine from a local medicine to a global commodity.

Opium use increased in the eighteenth century when medical authorities promoted the drug as a relief for a variety of conditions. Medical authorities started to promote cocaine in the nineteenth century, once the concentrated drug could be extracted from coca leaves. Many doctors claimed that cocaine would solve the problem of opiate addiction, because it would be used as a substitute for opiates. The curing of one addiction with a drug that causes a new addiction was a common idea when dealing with these drugs. Meanwhile, extensive marketing and mass production made them into global commodities by the nineteenth century. When we think about their addictive qualities, we may be tempted to conclude that the global spread of these two drugs was inevitable. And naturally, the addictive nature of these drugs and their users' dependence on them needs to be part of the discussion, since it was the strategies of producers, merchants, authorities, and consumers that increased the amount and availability of these drugs. Opium and cocaine are examples of this trend of industrialization and commercialization.

Opium and Cocaine Before the Eighteenth Century

Before it became a globalized commodity, people used opium grown locally. In Mesopotamia, farmers had cultivated opium since at least 3400 BCE. Cultivation of plant spread across Asia Minor into Africa, across the Balkans into Europe, and across the Middle East into India and Asia.[8] Medical authorities used the drug locally across these areas as a sedative, a light painkiller, and for other various illnesses, but in a limited fashion. Turkish and Arab traders first introduced opium to China in the late sixth or early seventh century. Users took the drug orally to relieve tension and pain, but its use in China was limited until the seventeenth century. A contributing reason for the spread of recreational opium is the belief among Chinese consumers that the drug increased sexual stamina and pleasure. Opium producers would reinforce this belief later in the nineteenth century as a method of increasing sales. The earliest clear description of this type of use came from Xu Boling, a scholar-official of the Ming Dynasty (1368–1644), who wrote in his book *Jingjing Juan* in 1483 that men "mainly used opium to aid masculinity, strengthen sperm and regain vigor," and that it "enhances the art of alchemists, sex and court ladies."[9] By 1578 Li Shizhen, a Ming Dynasty physician,

---

8. Booth, *Opium,* 15.

9. Yangwen Zheng, "The Social Life of Opium in China, 1483–1999." *Modern Asian Studies* 37, no. 1 (2003): 5.

listed standard medical uses of opium in his *Compendium of Materia Medica* and wrote that "lay people use it for the art of sex," in particular the ability to "arrest seminal emission."[10] Publishers printed the *Compendium* in Europe and many scholars consider it the most comprehensive treatment of traditional Chinese medicine at the time. By the seventeenth century smoking opium became more common, as by then many Chinese had adopted the belief that opium aided in sex. In the male-dominated culture of the Ming Dynasty, men adhered to this notion more than women, and men made up the majority of opium smokers.

Cocaine's widespread use developed more slowly. Before chemists developed cocaine South American indigenous peoples chewed coca leaves, containing the cocaine alkaloid, for thousands of years. When the Spanish arrived in South America, most ignored native claims that the leaf gave them strength and energy, as Spanish Christians considered the practice of chewing it the work of the devil. Later, after discovering the native claims had merit, Spanish authorities legalized and taxed the leaf. In 1569 Nicolás Monardes, a Spanish physician and botanist, described the practice of chewing a mixture of tobacco and coca leaves as inducing "great contentment": "When they [Native Americans] wished to make themselves drunk and out of judgment, they chewed a mixture of tobacco and coca leaves which make them go as they were out of their wittes."[11] In 1609 Padre Blas Valera, a priest from Lima, Peru wrote about coca leaves:

> Coca protects the body from many ailments, and our doctors use it in powdered form to reduce the swelling of wounds, to strengthen broken bones, to expel cold from the body or prevent it from entering, and to cure rotten wounds or sores that are full of maggots. And if it does so much for outward ailments, will not its singular virtue have even greater effect in the entrails of those who eat it?[12]

As can be seen from this account, local consumers used the drug for a variety of ailments. However, chewing coca leaves remained a local South American practice, as many people considered the leaves too bitter, and they also left the users with bad breath and stained teeth. Even though medical authorities found the leaves useful medicinally, few consumers used them. It would not be until the industrialized nineteenth century that the drug would increase in global demand.

The development of laudanum provided producers and consumers with a way to expand the medicinal use of opium. In the sixteenth century a Swiss physician,

10. Li Shizhen's book was published in various languages across Europe. Zheng, "Social Life of Opium," 6.

11. Steven B. Karch, *A Brief History of Cocaine* (Boston: CRC Press, 1998), 5.

12. Karch, *A Brief History of Cocaine*, 7.

alchemist, and astrologer known as Paracelsus (Theophrastus von Hohenheim) developed *Laudanum* as "tincture of opium," a solution of opium in alcohol.[13] Paracelsus challenged the theories and motives of contemporary medicine with chemical therapies, and discovered that opium dissolved in alcohol. He created a solution with 10 percent opium powder in alcohol, making consumption easier than mixing it with water, as it hid the bitter taste of the opium. In the 1660s Thomas Sydenham recommended laudanum for pain, sleeplessness, and diarrhea. Sydenham, a famed doctor in seventeenth-century England known as the "father of English medicine," believed that opium was "given to man by God to ease all suffering."[14] By 1728 the *Chambers Cyclopedia* (a universal dictionary of arts and sciences) listed opium as a cure-all, with laudanum being the most common form in the West. The listing of opium in the *Cyclopedia*, one of the first general encyclopedias in English, highlights the common usage of the drug by medical authorities of the time. Laudanum would become the basis of many common patent medicines of the nineteenth century, which will be examined later in the chapter. Why did consumers prefer laudanum over regular opium? Users normally mixed opium powder with water, but the bitter taste proved unacceptable except as a medical necessity. After Paracelsus developed laudanum and Sydenham promoted the mixture, producers discovered that alcohol masked the bitter taste of the opium, which made it much more palatable with consumers. Merchants promoted laudanum as a wonder drug that could cure anything, and use by consumers continued to increase. As can be seen in this example, available supply and promotion helped create demand. While opium use increased in Europe, the expansion of the opium market in China by European merchants elevated the drug to a global commodity. European merchants, especially the British, sought new markets and new ways to dominate the global trade networks. The sale of opium provided them the means to spread their influence and increase their profits.

Merchants started trading opium for medical use in the eighteenth century. Physicians used arsenic, mercuries, and various emetics for treatment, so using opium was a mild alternative in comparison. Opium causes constipation, so doctors used it as an effective treatment for the symptoms of cholera, dysentery, and diarrhea. They used the drug as a cough suppressant to treat bronchitis, tuberculosis, and other respiratory illnesses. It was also prescribed for rheumatism and insomnia.[15] While opium did not cure any of these conditions, patients took it because it alleviated their symptoms, and doctors promoted the drug as less

---

13. Barbara Hodgson, *In the Arms of Morpheus: The Tragic History of Morphine, Laudanum and Patent Medicines* (Richmond Hill, ON: Firefly Books, 2001), 45.

14. Booth, *Opium*, 27.

15. Marcus Aurin, "Chasing the Dragon: The Cultural Metamorphosis of Opium in the United States, 1825–1935," *Medical Anthropology Quarterly* 14, no. 3 (2000): 418.

harmful than other treatments. Medical authorities discovered opium to be a good remedy for nervous disorders as well, due to its calming effect. Doctors used it to quiet the minds of those with psychosis, to help people considered insane, and to treat patients with insomnia.[16] They noticed that in cases of psychosis, opium sometimes resulted in anger or depression, and it caused depressed patients to become more depressed after the effects wore off. Medical authorities also thought its usefulness outweighed its addictive qualities. The marketing of the drug as a cure-all created a larger demand for the drug, so merchants and producers worked on increasing production. As producers provided more opium, they continued to market the drug as major cure for a variety of conditions, which expanded its use. During the same time, many consumers still only used coca leaves at the local level.

Eighteenth-Century Trade Patterns

Portuguese merchants first became aware of the lucrative medicinal and recreational trade of opium into China in the late seventeenth century. Chinese consumers started smoking opium only after British traders introduced the practice of smoking North American tobacco in the seventeenth century. At first they mixed opium powder with tobacco, but then switched to smoking opium alone, and it soon became popular throughout China. British merchants attempted to establish tobacco markets in China, but as was explored in chapter 1, Chinese consumers preferred local Chinese tobacco over the British commodity produced in the American colonies.

Portuguese merchants realized that the new fashion of smoking of opium, combined with its reputation as a sexual aid, provided an opportunity for an expanded market to compete with the British. From various production areas across Asia, they supplied the port of Canton with opium to satisfy both the medicinal and recreational use of the drug. This allowed Portuguese merchants to expand their markets in China. Opium for smoking gave European merchants another product for the Chinese market, and the British would follow the Portuguese and start importing opium as well. When smoked opium has a far more potent narcotic effect, which increased sales.

Early in the eighteenth century the Portuguese imported opium from India and sold it in China for considerable profit. By 1729 Chinese authorities recognized addiction as a problem, so the Yung-cheng Emperor (r. 1722–1735) prohibited the sale and smoking of opium. However, similar to efforts to regulate other drugs explained in chapter 1, his ban failed to stop the trade. The major

---

16. John C. Kramer, "Opium Rampant: Medical Use, Misuse and Abuse in Britain and the West in the 17th and 18th Centuries," *British Journal of Addiction*.74, no. 4 (1979): 380.

difference between opium and the other drugs was that political authorities, when they did try to ban the drug, banned it due to the social costs of addiction and not because it was a political threat. The ban failed, as Chinese officials found it difficult to enforce due to lack of local support. Low-paid local officials accepted bribes from smugglers to increase their own income. Exporters continued to import opium into China, as the growing market provided them with lucrative profits. Merchants promoted the beliefs about its medicinal uses and sexual stimulation, and consumers continued to buy the drug. This highlights another example of the relationship between supply and demand. As increased opium use spread in China, some European traders started to explore the use of coca leaves and their potential as a new product.

The first botanical description of the coca plant appeared in 1580 in a book by Nicolas Monardes, a Spanish physician. However, the French botanist and explorer Joseph de Jussieu brought the first specimens of the plant to Europe for examination in 1750.[17] The managers of the Royal Botanical Gardens at Kew in southwest London quickly appreciated the commercial potential of the coca leaf.[18] The Lord Capel of Tewkesbury established the garden in 1721, but King George III expanded the garden to explore various plants from the British colonies that had economic potential, following the success of tobacco. After de Jussieu introduced the coca plants the Royal botanists brought them to the garden, but did little with them. Botanists would not seriously explore the commercial potential until Sir William Hooker, an English botanist, published a drawing of the plant in the Kew Gardens *Companion to the Botanical Magazine* in 1836.

While interest in coca developed slowly, the British merchants quickly moved into the opium trade with China in the 1730s due to Great Britain's trade imbalance with China, and they became the leading suppliers of the Chinese market. Chinese tea, silks, and porcelain pottery were desired across Europe, but the Chinese had little demand for Europe's manufactured goods and other trade items. This forced Great Britain to pay for Chinese products with silver. As a result, Great Britain's silver stocks decreased, so the British encouraged Chinese opium use to enhance their trade balance, and they imported it from Indian provinces under British control. In India, the British government provided the British East India Company (EIC) with a monopoly on cultivation, manufacture, and traffic of opium to China.[19] The EIC gained the power of *diwan* (government official) in Indian provinces of Bengal, Bihar, and Odisha after the

---

17. Lester Grinspoon and James B. Bakalar, *Cocaine: A Drug and Its Social Evolution* (New York: Basic Books, 1976), 18.

18. Karch, *Brief History of Cocaine*, 11.

19. Philip Lawson, *The East India Company: A History* (London: Routledge, 1993), 69.

1757 Battle of Plassey and the 1764 Battle of Buxar during the Seven Years' War (Map 2.1).[20] The company forced farmers to grow poppies using a combination of strong-arm tactics and debt (another feature of imperialism investigated in more detail in chapter 3). The EIC developed a method of growing opium poppies cheaply and abundantly. This strategy led to the increase of the land tax to 50 percent of the value of crops and to the doubling of East India Company profits by 1777.[21]

MAP 2.1 India, with East India Company Holdings, 1785

---

20. The Seven Years' War, a global conflict fought between 1756 and 1763, involved the major European powers of the time. The conflict spanned five continents, affecting Europe, the Americas, West Africa, India, and the Philippines.

21. Lawson, *The East India Company*, 72.

Other Western nations joined the trade, including the United States, which dealt in Turkish-grown as well as Indian-grown opium. The opium trade, which created a steady demand among Chinese addicts for opium imported by the West, solved this trade imbalance. Chinese consumers highly prized Bengal opium, which commanded twice the price of the domestic Chinese product, regarded as inferior in quality. The EIC did not always carry the opium itself, but due to the Chinese ban, employed private traders licensed by the company to take goods from India to China. These traders sold the opium to smugglers along the Chinese coast for gold and silver. The wealth the traders received from these sales were then turned over to the East India Company. In China, the company used the money to purchase goods such as tea that could be sold profitably in England.

The increased trade in opium allowed Britain to solve their trade imbalance and made the EIC large profits.[22] The amount of opium Europeans exported into China increased from around 200 chests (one chest equaled 65 kilograms) a year in 1729 to about 1,000 chests in 1767, with the East India Company shipping over two thousand chests into China in 1773. The company then tightened its grip on the opium trade by enforcing direct trade between opium farmers and the British, ending the role of Bengali purchasing agents. More available opium led to more use, which led to more addiction. Demand for the drug drove merchants to increase the supply, which in turn created more demand. As a result, the Qing dynasty Jiaqing Emperor issued an imperial decree banning imports of the drug in 1799. The edict failed, as by this time a network of opium distribution had formed throughout China, often via the connivance of corrupt officials. European merchants saw opium as a lucrative product, and Great Britain found a way to solve the trade balance problem by increasing opium importation in China during the nineteenth century. Due to the rise of mass production opium became a truly global commodity, exemplifying the growing globalization of the nineteenth century.

Industrialization and Global Commercialization

The industrial production of opium and cocaine increased with the advent of industrial agriculture. Industrialization not only affects manufacture but changes agricultural production as well. Agricultural development in England between the sixteenth century and the mid-nineteenth century saw a massive increase in productivity and net output. This supported population growth, freeing up a significant percentage of the workforce from farming, and supported the Industrial Revolution. The most important innovations included enclosure (the practice of combining small farms

22. Carl A. Trocki, *Opium, Empire and the Global Political Economy: A History of the Asian Opium Trade, 1750–1950* (London: Routledge, 2005), 86.

into large landholdings), mechanization, four-field crop rotation, and selective breeding.[23] Farmers in the British colonies in North America transferred many of these techniques to the colonies, but outside of the Southern colonies, farmers operated family farms. In the Southern colonies, large slave plantations growing tobacco developed by imitating the sugar plantations of the Caribbean. Meanwhile in India, the British exported only few crops to the world market, including opium. In the early nineteenth century, with the development of industrial agriculture, agricultural techniques, implements, seed stocks, and cultivars improved, which created a yield per land unit many times that of the Middle Ages.[24] The development of industrial agriculture impacted the production of opium poppies and coca leaves as well. However, both opium and coca harvesting could only be mechanized to a degree, so producers still relied heavily on manual labor to produce the crops. The increased production of the crops, combined with mass production and scientific advancements, created larger quantities of opium and cocaine products.

English producers used industrial agriculture methods to produce more opium in India for export to China. By 1804 Great Britain's trade deficit with China had turned into a surplus, leading to seven million dollars in silver going to Britain between 1806 and 1809.[25] The increased importation caused the Chinese government to attempt to halt the opium trade again. In 1804 the emperor issued a further imperial edict:

> Opium has a harm. Opium is a poison, undermining our good customs and morality. Its use is prohibited by law. . . . However, recently the purchasers, eaters, and consumers of opium have become numerous. Deceitful merchants buy and sell it to gain profit. . . . If we confine our search for opium to the seaports, we fear the search will not be sufficiently thorough. We should also order the general commandant of the police and police- censors at the five gates to prohibit opium and to search for it at all gates. If they capture any violators, they should immediately punish them and should destroy the opium at once. . . . the provinces from which opium comes, we order their viceroys, governors, and superintendents of the maritime customs to conduct a thorough search for opium and cut off its supply. They should in no ways consider this order a dead letter and allow opium to be smuggled out![26]

---

23. Mark Overton, *Agricultural Revolution in England* (Cambridge: Cambridge University Press, 2010), 34.

24. Noel Kingsbury, *Hybrid: The History and Science of Plant Breeding* (Chicago: University of Chicago Press, 2009), 28.

25. David Edward Owen, *British Opium Policy in China and India* (New Haven, CT: Yale University Press, 1968), 66.

26. Lo-Shu Fu, *A Documentary Chronicle of Sino-Western Relations,* Vol. 1 (Tucson: University of Arizona Press, 1966), 380.

As we can see from this excerpt, the emperor believed opium to be a major threat to China, and that local officials were not doing enough to stop the trade. But the decree had little effect, since the Qing government in Beijing could not halt opium smuggling in the southern provinces where they had little stable control. A porous Chinese border and increasing local demand facilitated the trade as well.

Between 1820 and 1830, British merchants imported around 10,000 chests of opium per year. The balance of payments continued to run against China and in favor of Britain, which increased the British support of the trade. While Britain dominated the trade, some competition came from the newly independent United States. Leading American traders John Cushing, Robert Bennet Forbes, and John Jacob Astor sold Turkish opium in the Chinese province of Guangzhou in the 1820s.[27] Cushing—working for the James and Thomas H. Perkins Company of Boston—smuggled Turkish opium into the port city of Canton. Robert Bennet Forbes worked for Russell and Co., one of the largest American opium shippers. John Jacob Astor's American Fur Company smuggled tons of opium into Canton before being forced out of the business by the East India Company.

Portuguese traders also brought opium from the independent Malwa states of western India, and opium prices dropped due to this competition. The trade in opium now represented a global enterprise, as the East India Company processed opium at its factories in the cities of Patna and Benares in North India for shipment to China. Due to the dropping prices, they increased production in an attempt to move the product into more areas of China and overwhelm Portuguese production.[28] This is another example of strategic supply to increase demand. By 1820, the British restricted the Portuguese trade by charging "pass duty" on the opium as it passed through Bombay (which the British controlled) to reach a port.[29] In 1838 European merchants imported 40,000 chests into China annually, the majority shipped by the EIC. Despite drastic penalties and continued prohibition of opium until 1860, opium importation rose steadily over the years. Opium smuggling provided 15 to 20 percent of the British Empire's revenue and at the same time caused a silver shortage in China. Companies such as the EIC helped make opium a major part of global commerce by promoting the drug across China; however, the expanding Industrial Revolution and mass production profoundly affected the global trade.

---

27. Hunt Janin, *The India-China Opium Trade in the Nineteenth Century* (London: McFarland & Company, 1999), 63.

28. Maggie Keswick and Clara Weatherall, *The Thistle and the Jade: A Celebration of 175 Years of Jardine Matheson* (London: Frances Lincoln, 2008), 78.

29. Trocki, *Opium, Empire and the Global Political Economy*, 79.

The Industrial Revolution

As a driving force behind the spread of global commerce in the nineteenth century, the Industrial Revolution transformed society from a primarily agricultural one into one based on the manufacturing of goods and services. Producers often replaced physical labor with more mechanized mass production and assembly lines. Industrialization led to technological advancements, which in turn helped create surplus. Producers needed to expand their markets in order to sell the surplus (i.e., expand demand). Trade relationships grew, which led to the expansion of globalization. More people bought a greater variety of textiles, clothing, shoes, and household and domestic items, including ceramics, cutlery, mirrors, books, clocks, furniture, curtains, and bedding. Mass production of small items also included buckles, ribbons, buttons, snuff boxes, and other fancy goods. Industrial agriculture impacted consumers as they purchased beer, butter, bread, milk, meat, vegetables, fruit, fish, and other foodstuffs that they no longer produced at home.

Changes in manufacturing impacted individual families' food choices as well. During the mid-nineteenth century, canned food became a status symbol among middle-class households in Europe and the United States, and a cheaper source of food for working-class families. Population growth in Europe and an increasingly mechanized canning process resulted in a rising demand for canned food. By the 1860s new inventions and improvements led to smaller machine-made steel cans and faster production. Demand for canned food also greatly increased during large-scale wars in the nineteenth century—the Crimean War, the American Civil War, and the Franco-Prussian War—which introduced increasing numbers of working-class men to canned food. Canning companies expanded their businesses to meet military demands for nonperishable food, allowing companies to manufacture in bulk and sell to wider civilian markets after wars ended. Urban populations demanded ever-increasing quantities of cheap, varied quality food that they could keep at home without having to go shopping daily. All of these types of manufactured goods had a profound impact on peoples' daily lives. The techniques developed for mass canned food production extended into the manufacture of products containing drugs as well.

As an aspect of this expansion, opium began to be produced in larger quantities for medicinal use. The development and mass production of morphine offers an example of the industrialization of opium. Friedrich Sertürner, a German scientist, discovered morphine as the first active alkaloid extracted from the opium poppy in 1804.[30] He tested the new drug on three young boys, who almost died, but Sertürner realized that the correct dosage put them into a deep sleep.

---

30. David Courtwright, *Forces of Habit: Drugs and the Making of the Modern World* (Cambridge, MA: Harvard University Press, 2001), 36.

Sertürner named it *morphium* after the Greek god of dreams, Morpheus. Due to Sertürner's experiments, physicians believed that opium had finally been perfected and tamed. They lauded morphine as "God's own medicine" for its reliability, long-lasting effects, and safety. Producers promoted morphine as a safer alternative to opium in the West, while still promoting opium's use in China. Why promote morphine as a safer alternative to opium in the West but not in China? There were growing concerns about the safety of prolonged opium use in European countries, to which merchants paid heed, as it would impact their legal business. Chinese authorities had already banned opium, but the smuggling of the drug continued to be a profitable enterprise under a weakened Chinese government. In 1817 Sertürner and Company first marketed morphine to the general public as a pain medication, and also as a treatment for opium and alcohol addiction. Medical authorities commonly treated addiction with other addictive drugs, as stated earlier. Pharmacies and doctors promoted the new drug in order to quiet fears about the addictive nature of opium, and sales increased. The increase in sales led to the increase of commercial production.

In 1827, morphine supplies increased as production began in the German Confederation by the pharmacy that later became the now-behemoth pharmaceutical company Merck. With the discovery of morphine, and the overall benefits of using it to relieve pain after surgery, it became widely used in the medical profession. In 1847, Dr. Alexander Wood of Edinburgh perfected a type of syringe to administer morphine, as he discovered that injection increased the effects, making narcotic qualities almost instantaneous and three times more potent.[31] Doctors used morphine, along with opium and laudanum, in the Crimean War (1853–1856) and the American Civil War (1861–1865) to relieve pain after surgical procedures performed in field hospitals.[32] The sedative effect of morphine allowed Civil War doctors to ensure that patients could get the rest that was necessary for recovery. Morphine's use during these wars established the drug as a major painkiller that could be purchased over the counter in any pharmacy. The reputation of morphine, the perfection of hypodermic needles, and the addictive quality of the drug all contributed to the spread and increase in morphine sales. As we move into the late nineteenth century, merchants and consumers made opiates a major part of the global economy, which fully integrated opium products into societies around the world.

As demand for new types of medicines increased, doctors started to explore the uses of coca leaves more fully in the early nineteenth century. Although some botanists knew the stimulant and hunger-suppressant properties of coca, it was not

31. Hodgson, *In the Arms of Morpheus*, 80.

32. Virginia Berridge and Griffin Edwards, *Opium and the People: Opiate Use in Nineteenth Century England* (New Haven, CT: Yale University Press, 1987), 136.

favored due to the need to chew the leaves. After 1825, travelers from all over Europe visited the new South American republics and came in contact with the practice of chewing coca leaves, which increased the scientific interest.[33] Various European scientists attempted to isolate cocaine but did not succeed due to the insufficient knowledge of chemistry at the time; shipping conditions were also an issue, as they degraded the cocaine in the plant samples available. Interest waned until Sir William Hooker published his drawings in *Companion to the Botanical Magazine* in 1836. The combination of the interest generated by the wave of travelers to South America, and the published drawing, brought coca to the attention of scientists again. As industrial chemistry improved, scientists started working on the coca leaf. Friedrich Gaedcke a German chemist first isolated the cocaine alkaloid in 1855. Gaedcke named the alkaloid "erythroxyline" and published a description in the journal *Archiv der Pharmazie*. In 1859 Albert Niemann, a German PhD student at the University of Göttingen, received a trunk full of fresh coca from South America and developed an improved purification process, naming the alkaloid "cocaine."[34]

After Niemann published his findings, which earned him his doctorate, the Merck Pharmaceutical Company started to produce experimental commercial batches of cocaine. Then in 1859 Paolo Mantegazza, an Italian doctor, after witnessing first-hand the use of coca by the local indigenous peoples in Peru, proceeded to experiment on himself and wrote a paper in which he described the effects. In this paper he declared coca and cocaine useful medicinally, in the treatment of "a furred tongue in the morning, flatulence, and whitening of the teeth."[35] This paper added additional support for the use of cocaine. Historian Joseph Spillane argues that cocaine was the first "modern" drug—that is, although plant-based, its discovery, profile, and applications all derived from evolving laboratory science.[36] The modernizing and industrial pharmaceutical firms used-cutting edge science of the time to develop the drug. The urban Western culture of the mid-nineteenth century was characterized by rapid industrialization and modernization of everyday life. This changing culture offered an arena for commercial producers to promote a new, miraculous energy-enhancing stimulant. By the mid-nineteenth century consumers adopted coffee, tea, sugar, and tobacco as regular commodities, and merchants desired something exotic to open up new markets. Cocaine, and the increasing use of opiates, provided these products.

33. Paul Gootenberg, *Andean Cocaine: The Making of a Global Drug* (Chapel Hill: University of North Carolina Press, 2008), 21.

34. Gootenberg, *Andean Cocaine*, 22.

35. Joseph Kennedy, *Coca Exotica: The Illustrated Story of Cocaine* (Madison, NJ: Fairleigh Dickinson University Press, 1985), 57.

36. Joseph F. Spillane, "Making a Modern Drug: The Manufacture, Sale, and Control of Cocaine in the United States, 1880–1920," in *Cocaine: Global Histories*, ed. Paul Gootenberg (London: Routledge, 1999), 23.

By the middle of the nineteenth century, the Chinese economy depended on opium as merchants used the drug as a substitute for cash. Businesses accepted it in the interior provinces of China, as it weighed less than copper coins. China's attempts to stop the flood of opium into the country led to two wars with the British government. The two Opium Wars in China demonstrate the role of imperialism in the increasingly globalized drug trade.

Following China's defeat in the Second Opium War in 1860, the British government forced the Chinese government to legalize opium and began massive domestic production as part of the peace settlement.[37] Why would Britain prefer to grow opium poppies in China instead of India? Demonstrating the interconnection of commercialization and imperialism, British opium merchants decided that they needed to save transportation costs. They moved the main production from India to China, due to the location of the major markets there. Since poppies could be grown in almost any soil or weather, cultivation started to spread across China. In China's stagnating economy, opium supplied fluid capital and created new sources of taxes.[38] Smugglers, poor farmers, retail merchants, and officials all depended on opium for their livelihood. Local officials met their tax quotas by relying on poppy growers even in areas where other crops were not doing well. A provincial governor observed that the government treated opium, once regarded as a poison, in the same way as tea or rice. By the 1880s, even governors who had initially suppressed opium smoking and poppy production now depended on opium taxes. British importation of opium peaked in 1879 at 6,700 tons, as production of opium in China started to dominate. The global trade in opium continued to increase as chemists developed more powerful drugs from opium.

During this same period, many entrepreneurs became interested in the potential of coca and cocaine to become a wonder drug and a global commodity in same fashion as opium. Angelo Mariani, a Corsican chemist, read Mantegazza's paper and became intrigued with coca and its economic potential. In 1863 Mariani marketed Vin Mariani, a wine treated with coca leaves, following the concept of opium and alcohol. The ethanol in wine extracted the cocaine alkaloid from the coca leaves, altering the drink's effect. Vin Mariani contained 7.2 mg of cocaine per ounce.[39] He advertised the wine as a tonic stimulant for "fatigued and overworked body and brain" and as a treatment for malaria, influenza, and all wasting diseases. Doctors in the nineteenth century lacked a full understanding of medical knowledge and often used dangerous and crude treatments. Cocaine does not cure any of these diseases, but provided energy and relief from symptoms, so medical authorities promoted use of the drug.

---

37. Janin, *The India-China Opium Trade*, 106.

38. Jonathan Spence, *Chinese Roundabout: Essays in History and Culture* (New York: Norton, 1992), 251.

39. Gootenberg, *Andean Cocaine*, 25.

As cocaine started to become more usable in the late nineteenth century, manufacturers started to explore whether a more powerful but nonaddictive opium product could be developed. Mass production of drugs in the Industrial Revolution gave manufacturers the impetus to create new drugs for the market. Chemists produced nitrous oxide, ether, and chloroform, while companies mass-produced mild painkillers (aspirin), anti-fever treatments, anti-toxins, and made strides in the use of vaccines.

This also led to the development of heroin. C. R. Alder Wright, an English chemist, synthesized diamorphine (heroin) in 1874 by combining morphine with various acids.[40] Wright's invention did not lead to any further developments, and diamorphine only became prominent when Felix Hoffman resynthesized it twenty years later. Hoffmann, working at Bayer pharmaceutical company in Elberfeld, Germany, experimented with morphine to find a less potent and less addictive product. In 1895, Bayer marketed morphine as an over-the-counter drug under the trademark name "heroin."[41] They developed it as a morphine substitute for cough suppressants, arguing that it did not have morphine's addictive side effects. The development of heroin increased the demand for raw opium, adding impetus to the expansion of production in China. In 1879 doctors also began to use cocaine to treat morphine addiction. Once again, doctors used addictive drugs to solve the problem of addiction. Medical professionals during this period had a limited knowledge of the long-term effects of these drugs. They conducted few studies, and in their drive to find a new wonder drug, promoted solutions that they did not fully research or understand. Bayer thought they had a nonaddictive substitute for morphine to market (See Figure 2.1). However, contrary to Bayer's advertising as a nonaddictive morphine substitute, heroin soon had one of the highest rates of addiction among its users. This did not stop the spread of heroin commercially, as it became one of the major Bayer products.

A similar pattern occurred with cocaine. Physicians introduced cocaine into clinical use as a local anesthetic in Germany in 1884, and a year later Sigmund Freud published his work *Über Coca*. Freud believed that cocaine would prove a valuable therapeutic for addiction, depression, and neurasthenia, an exhausting condition defined by late nineteenth-century physicians as a type of nerve-cell fatigue. He fully supported cocaine use and became a regular user as well. He wrote that cocaine causes:

exhilaration and lasting euphoria, which in no way differs from the normal euphoria of the healthy person. You perceive an increase of self-control and possess more vitality and capacity for work. In other words, you are

40. Booth, *Opium*, 77.

41. Booth, *Opium*, 77.

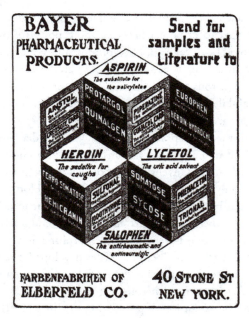

FIGURE 2.1 1898 Bayer Heroin advertisement. By the end of the nineteenth century heroin, made from raw opium produced in China, was a major product.
Source: Bayer ad – Bettmann/Getty Images.

simply normal, and it is soon hard to believe you are under the influence of any drug. Long intensive physical work is performed without any fatigue. This result is enjoyed without any of the unpleasant after-effects that follow exhilaration brought about by alcoholic beverages. No craving for the further use of cocaine appears after the first, or even after repeated taking of the drug.[42]

Freud's promotion of cocaine as a wonder drug for a variety of conditions aided in the opinion of cocaine as a cure-all. Manufacturers mass-produced cocaine as well as opiates, and they became the drugs of choice for the nineteenth century.

All of this promotion by doctors, pharmaceutical companies, and chemists helped form a global market for cocaine. This global boom in German and American medicinal and consumer cocaine would not have been feasible without the active participation of South Americans. This participation included the Peruvian landowners and peasants who planted, tended, and expanded coca fields, as well as the pharmacy and factory entrepreneurs who built a new industry

---

42. Markel, *An Anatomy of Addiction*, 81.

from scratch after 1885. All local production increased in order to supply over-seas drug companies like Merck.[43] Coca leaves, Peru's fastest growing export by the 1890s, developed into a full global commodity.

Coca leaves exported mainly to US markets grew from 300 tons in 1890 to over 11,000 tons by 1905. While this trade dominated the market, Peru also de-veloped its own industrial production of cocaine. Alfredo Bignon, a Peruvian scientist who emigrated from France, developed a simple formula for cocaine production. Bignon's refining technique spurred the creation of crude cocaine processing factories in Lima. American and German traders preferred shipping the semiprocessed cocaine over the bulkier coca leaves. This afforded Peru a stronger position in the global trade of the commodity. However, by the early twentieth century American and German manufacturers dominated the cocaine trade and relegated Peru to a secondary position of production, which will be ex-amined further in chapter 3. In order to understand the growing demand and use of opium and cocaine we need to examine the mass production and promotion of these drugs that drove their globalization.

Mass Production and Advertising: Patent Medicines and Coca-Cola

Mass production increased during the Second Industrial Revolution (1880–1920), which consisted of rapid industrialization in the later part of the nineteenth century and the early twentieth century. By the middle of the nineteenth century, industrial areas firmly established machine-assisted manufacture, the division of labor and standardization. Large factories operated on both sides of the Atlantic, and some industries, such as textiles and steel, used advanced processes, machin-ery, and equipment. The rapid expansion of rail, barge, ship, and road transpor-tation accelerated the growth of manufacturing. The new transport companies allowed factories to obtain raw materials and to ship finished products over increasingly large distances, but they also created a substantial demand for the output of the new products and markets. The enormous expansion of rail and telegraph lines after 1870 created an increase in the movement of people and ideas, which led to a new wave of globalization. An interrelationship between iron, steel, railroads, and coal also developed at the beginning of the Second Industrial Revolution. Railroads, using cheap coal, created cheap transportation of materials and products, which led to cheap rails to build more roads. All of this expanded the mass production of a myriad of products and increased the spread of globalization, and the supplies of opium and cocaine followed suit.

---

43. Gootenberg, *Andean Cocaine*, 62.

Manufacturers mass-produced opiates, as industrialization allowed for laudanum to be used in a wide variety of products. The nineteenth century saw widespread use of laudanum in Europe and the United States. As an example, the wife of President Abraham Lincoln, Mary Todd Lincoln, suffered from laudanum addiction.[44] Doctors prescribed laudanum for ailments, from colds to cardiac diseases to meningitis in both adults and children. Many doctors prescribed the drug to large numbers of nineteenth-century women for relief of menstrual cramps and vague aches. Nurses fed laudanum to infants. At first, the working class used the drug since it cost less than a bottle of gin or wine, because governments did not tax medicine. After the 1860s, various companies used laudanum in many patent medicines to relieve pain, produce sleep, and to cure a variety of symptoms. Producers created patent medicines as proprietary (i.e., with a "secret formula") and unproved remedies were advertised and sold directly to the public. Many patent medicines contained laudanum, but others used cannabis, cocaine, and a variety of other chemicals. Consumers in the United States found these remedies very attractive. The patent medicine industry in the United States spread due to the medical shortcomings of the early nineteenth century. Many patients had limited access to doctors, and they cost more than the average worker in America could afford. Knowledge of human physiology and of the causes and progress of disease was also extremely limited. Louis Pasteur first published germ theory in 1861, but it would take years to be widespread knowledge among doctors. The mother of the family generally provided healthcare, relying on home remedies. However, these home remedies could not combat the terrible diseases that became endemic during the course of the nineteenth century—typhoid, typhus, yellow fever, and cholera. The fear of these diseases directly led to the success of the patent medicine industry.[45]

Before industrialization housewives and grandmothers supplied their friends and relations with homemade remedies, but with mass production entrepreneurs with business savvy began to bottle and sell old family recipes. If the recipe became a commercial success, bottling factories appeared, then networks of traveling salesmen, followed by distribution systems for wholesaling the product's increasing supply. Medicine-making became big business with the growth of the patent medicine industry, encouraged by a number of political, social, and economic factors. The expansion of public elementary schools meant that more people could read newspaper ads that promised cures and provided testimonials. Many people craved news from the front during the Civil War,

---

44. Anne E. Beidler, *The Addiction of Mary Todd Lincoln* (Seattle: Coffetown Press, 2009), 15.

45. James Harvey Young, *The Toadstool Millionaires: A Social History of Patent Medicines in America before Federal Regulation* (Princeton, NJ: Princeton University Press, 2015), 28.

which meant that more Americans read newspapers, giving patent medicine manufacturers access to more customers. Printers had access to cheap wood pulp paper and with improvements in the printing process, this meant that advertising volume could grow.[46] Newspapers ads promised quick, easy, inexpensive sure-cures for diseases both dreadful and mundane, such as Mrs. Winslow's Soothing Syrup (See Figure 2.2).

Following the Civil War, expanding settlement in the American West spurred additional advertising and marketing. Homesteaders, often isolated and unable to obtain professional medical help to combat diseases such as pneumonia, dysentery, and malaria, relied heavily on patent medicines.[47] Patent medicine manufacturers increased their advertising, and seeking a national market, they went directly to consumers using a variety of psychological lures. Many Americans suffered from dyspepsia, a common disease in the nineteenth century due to a poor diet. European visitors to America often commented

FIGURE 2.2 Ad for Mrs. Winslow's Soothing Syrup, which contained opium. Companies promoted it as teething aid for children.
Source: Mrs. Winslow's Soothing Syrup for children teething. Card. N. Y.: M. M. & O, Lith., 1870. Digital Commonwealth, https://ark.digitalcommonwealth.org/ark:/50959/8k71nj083 (accessed May 04, 2020).

---

46. Eric Jameson, *The Natural History of Quackery* (London: Michael Joseph, 1961), 46.

47. Young, *The Toadstool Millionaires,* 79.

on the American habit of gobbling enormous amounts of starch, salt, and fat. Manufacturers such as Dr. E. Rowell's Invigorating Tonic and Family Medicine guaranteed a cure from the condition. The opium laced product promised it would solve "impure blood, dyspepsia, indigestion, constipation, loss of appetite, biliousness, headache, jaundice, loss of memory, piles, eruptions of the skin, general debility, rheumatism, and all diseases arising from disordered liver, bowels or kidneys."[48]

Dr. Ayer of Lowell, Massachusetts, realized the potential for patent medicines in the American West. He increased his advertising and by 1870, he had contracts with 1,900 newspapers and periodicals and his factories produced 630,000 doses of Ayer remedies, the best-selling being Ayer's Cherry Pectoral for children. Others, such as Dr. Thomas' Eclectric Oil, which contained opium, alcohol, and chloroform, advertised that it would positively cure "toothache in 5 minutes, earache in 2 minutes, backache in 2 hours, lameness in 2 days, coughs in 20 minutes, hoarseness in 1 hour, colds in 24 hours, sore throat in 12 hours, deafness in 2 days, pain by burn in 5 minutes, pain of scald in 5 minutes."[49] Winslow's Soothing Syrup, advertised to help teething children, contained opiates in the proportion of one-half a gram of morphine to one and a half ounces of syrup plus a half-ounce of water, mixed with alcohol. Lloyd's Manufacturing Company produced another product to deal with toothaches, and the use of their Cocaine Toothache Drops became widespread. Dentists used cocaine as a regular product to deal with pain and recommended it for simple dental work. While cocaine appeared in several products, patent medicines became the common and very accepted method to spread the sales of opiates, increasing this lucrative trade. Many of the manufacturers became very wealthy. Among the most successful was Dr. Kilmer, who amassed a fortune estimated in the 1890s at 10 to 15 million.[50] The enormous profits in the patent medicine industry led to the formation of conglomerates, as businessmen amassed a product line of over 50 proprietary medicines. A witness before a Congressional committee in 1906 estimated that there were 50,000 patent medicines being made and sold in the United States.

By the 1880s consumers used cocaine regularly for a variety of conditions, with manufacturers producing the drug in large quantities for mass consumption. In 1885 the US manufacturer Parke-Davis sold cocaine in various forms, including in cigarettes, as a powder, and as a cocaine mixture for injection with the included needle. The company promised that its cocaine products would "supply

---

48. Jameson, *The Natural History of Quackery*, 82.

49. Jameson, *The Natural History of Quackery*, 85.

50. Young, *The Toadstool Millionaires,* 101.

the place of food, make the coward brave, the silent eloquent and render the sufferer insensitive to pain."[51] Parke-Davis promoted the drug as a diet aid, pain reliever, and all-around stimulant.

What became one of the largest selling cocaine drinks, Coca-Cola, entered the market as an alternative to coca wines and patent medicines. Confederate Colonel John Pemberton, wounded in the American Civil War, became a morphine addict. He turned to cocaine as a substitute, and created a prototype Coca-Cola recipe with coca leaves at Pemberton's Eagle Drug and Chemical House, a drugstore in Columbus, Georgia.[52] Inspired by the success of Vin Mariani, a French coca wine, in 1885 Pemberton registered his French Wine Cocanerve tonic.[53] In 1886, Atlanta and Fulton County, Georgia passed prohibition legislation, forcing Pemberton to develop Coca-Cola as a nonalcoholic version of French coca wine. He started selling his new drink at Jacob's Pharmacy in Atlanta on May 8, 1886, as a patent medicine for five cents a glass, adding kola nut and a lot of sugar.[54] Pemberton claimed that Coca-Cola cured morphine addiction, indigestion, nerve disorders, headaches, and impotence. His product did not sell well at first and in 1887, another Atlanta pharmacist and businessman, Asa Chandler, bought the formula for Coca-Cola from Pemberton for $2,300. Pemberton died in 1888, and Chandler would make the product a success. By the late 1890s, Coca-Cola was one of America's most popular fountain drinks, largely due to Chandler's aggressive marketing of the product. With Asa Chandler now in charge, the Coca-Cola Company increased syrup sales by over 4,000 percent between 1890 and 1900. At this time merchants sold Coca-Cola as a syrup that was mixed in pharmacies and soda fountains, and not bottled. Chandler continued to sell Coca-Cola as a tonic medicine until 1898, when the US government decided to start taxing medicines. Chandler then advertised the drink as a soda to avoid the new taxes. Chandler's continued use of aggressive advertising led to the drink being sold across the United States and Canada.

By 1890 over a hundred different beverages were being sold that contained coca extract or cocaine. In 1903 cocaine consumption increased to about five times that of 1890, predominately by nonmedical users. Employers provided the drug to industrial laborers as a stimulant to increase productivity. Cocaine was promoted among workers in factories, textile mills, and on railroads, where it supplemented or replaced caffeine as the drug of choice to keep

---

51. Spillane, "The making of a Modern Drug," 26.

52. Bartow J. Elmore, *Citizen Coke: The Making of Coca-Cola Capitalism* (New York: Norton, 2015), 20.

53. Mark Pendergrast, *For God Country and Coca-Cola* (New York: Basic Books, 2000), 25.

54. Bartow, *Citizen Coke*, 21.

workers awake and working overtime.[55] Attitudes on the use of cocaine started to change, as reformers and various authorities noted an increase in accidents and addiction.

By 1906 China produced 85 percent of the world's opium, some 35,000 tons, and 27 percent of its adult male population regularly used opium, equaling 13.5 million people.[56] Purified morphine and heroin became widely available for injection and patent medicines containing opiates reached a peak in recreational use. At this point various governments and reformers started to see the inherent social problems of the opium trade. Many countries prohibited opium and cocaine during the early twentieth century, leading to the modern application of opium production as a precursor for illegal recreational drugs or tightly regulated legal prescription drugs. We will discuss the prohibition of opium and cocaine in more detail in chapter 4.

As we can see, opium and cocaine moved from locally used products to a widespread global commodity due to industrialization and commercialization. Clearly addiction is a factor, but the increased use of these drugs cannot be seen as an inevitable consequence of addiction. Medical officials, producers, and commercial suppliers created and increased a demand for these drugs. Suppliers advertised opiates and cocaine as wonder drugs to cure a variety of conditions. Companies actively and intentionally promoted them in order to increase sales and expand markets. The Industrial Revolution led to the mass production of these drugs as well as other commodities, and the shift to industrial agriculture increased the supply of the plants. By examining the complex interplay between supply and demand of opiates and cocaine, we can shed light on the process of globalization. Does an increase in demand increase the supply? Or is the opposite true? While increasing demand is part of the process, it is also clear that an increasing supply of these two drugs resulted in producers and businesses working together to increase demand and expand their markets.

The globalization of opium and cocaine was not an inevitable process, but a conscious and determined choice made by producers, suppliers, and consumers. By examining the choices and their outcomes we can gain a better understanding of the role of industrialization and commercialization in the creation of modern globalization, which led to the mass production and consumption of these drugs. However, this is still only part of the story. Another aspect alluded to in this chapter is the role of politics and imperialism in this process. The expansion of imperialism in the nineteenth century, driven by the demand of the Industrial Revolution, played an independent role in the spread

---

55. Spillane, "Making of a Modern Drug," 93.

56. Berridge, *Opium and the People*, 223.

of globalization—not only of opium and cocaine, but of tobacco and coffee as well. We will explore the role of nineteenth-century imperialism and its impact in chapter 3. The interrelationship between industrialization, commercialization, and imperialism provides a lens for understanding of the process of modern globalization.

FURTHER READING

Bauer, Rolf. *The Peasant Production of Opium in Nineteenth-Century India*. Leiden: Brill Academic, 2019.

Burhop, Carsten. "Pharmaceutical Research in Wilhelmine Germany: The Case of E. Merck." *Business History Review* 83, no. 3 (2009): 475–503.

Gootenberg, Paul, ed. *Cocaine: Global Histories*. London: Routledge, 1999.

Hodgson, Barbara. *In the Arms of Morpheus: The Tragic History of Morphine, Laudanum and Patent Medicines*. Richmond Hill, ON: Firefly Books, 2001.

Zheng, Yangwen. "The Social Life of Opium in China, 1483–1999." *Modern Asian Studies* 37, no. 1 (2003): 1–39.

3 THE GLOBALIZATION OF DRUGS THROUGH IMPERIALISM

In 1832 William Napier, a Scottish representative in the House of Lords, lost his seat and needed to find other employment. A year later an opportunity appeared—he applied for the new position of Superintendent of British Trade in China. The British government created the ambassadorial-level position to replace the Select Committee of the East India Company, which lost its monopoly in China in 1833. Suddenly, China became central to the economy of Britain, whose government needed a permanent position to oversee the trade and economic ties. The British government believed that the previous trade with China had been untidy, if not downright chaotic. Napier received the position because no other qualified candidates applied, and due to his close connection, he asked King William IV to intervene.[1] Napier, after receiving Britain's first official resident posting in China, needed to maintain a legal tea trade financed by illegal drug imports. The new superintendent's solution was simply to blast China into submission. He wrote is his diary:

> The Empire of China is my own. What a glorious thing it wd [would] be to have a blockading squadron on the Coast of the Celestial Empire . . . how easily a gun brig [war ship] wd [would] raise a revolution and cause them to open their ports to the trading world. I would like to be the medium of such a change.[2]

Napier concluded that the key to British interest in China centered on tea and that violence or the threat of violence benefitted British interests. He stated that "Britain must be willing to use force."[3] What can we learn from Napier's attitude? By the time of his death in 1834, he had succeeded in moving Anglo-Chinese relations toward the

---

1. Julia Lovell, *The Opium War: Drugs, Dreams and the Making of Modern China* (New York: Overlook Press, 2015), 5.

2. Glenn Melancon, *Britain's China Policy and the Opium Crisis: Balancing Drugs, Violence and National Honor, 1833–1840* (Farnham, UK: Ashgate, 2003), 35.

3. Quoted in Priscilla Napier, *Barbarian Eye: Lord Napier in China* (London: Brassy's, 2003), 88.

possibility of armed conflict by replacing peaceful pragmatism with economic self-interest and pompous national principle. He also helped recast the British impulse toward war as a moral obligation. Napier's actions represent the growing dominance of an imperial mindset in Great Britain.

In chapter 2 we examined the nineteenth-century economic globalization of opium and cocaine through the processes of industrialization and commercialization. However, that was only a portion of the story: imperialism was just as powerful of a force as capitalism in the spread of modern globalization. Imperialism represents a shift from a focus on corporate interests to a more formal governmental interest. So what is imperialism? Imperialism is a policy or ideology extending a country's rule or domination over foreign nations through military force, or by political or economic control. After the Industrial Revolution, imperialism became a common practice of European nations seeking new sources of raw materials and markets to sell manufactured products. We need to understand that a major aspect of imperialism was the spread of industrial capitalism. Industrial powers sought to dominate resources and markets to bolster their capitalist economies. Industrialized countries sought to expand their economies by obtaining raw materials, which could be transported back to factories, turned into manufactured goods, and shipped back to the colonial markets for sale. This exchange increased the spread of modern globalization in the nineteenth century, since this commerce became increasingly global. Europeans started building empires in North and South America in the early 1500s, but by the early nineteenth century, Spain and Portugal's power had declined and many of their colonies had achieved independence. Britain, France, Germany, Russia, and the Netherlands continued to colonize during this period, and they spread their empires in several ways. Japan and the United States also joined the European nations in the late nineteenth century as imperial powers.

How does imperialism apply to the spread of coffee, tobacco, rum, opium, and cocaine? Producers and merchants spread these commodities not only through industrialization and commercialization, but also with governmental aid through imperialism. A driving force behind imperialism was the increasing industrialization of the nineteenth and early twentieth centuries. The governments of the industrial capitalist nations supported commercialization and industrialization to strengthen their economies and enhance their power. In this chapter we will explore the role of coffee, tobacco, and rum in the imperialism of the early nineteenth century, and the spread of opium and cocaine in relation to the second wave of imperialism of the late nineteenth and early twentieth centuries. We also need to keep in mind that what we explored in chapter 2 occurred at the same time and was intertwined with what we will discuss in this chapter. Industrial capitalism and imperialism are two sides of the same coin, being completely interlaced. We will begin the examination with the spread of coffee, tobacco, and rum in the early nineteenth century, as it highlights the spread of imperialism and its role in globalization.

Drugs and Early Imperialism

In chapter 1, we saw that French merchants used African and indigenous slave labor to produce coffee for export in Martinique and Saint-Domingue (Haiti). The latter supplied half the world's coffee by 1788, just three years before the slave rebellion overthrew the existing colonial order on the island. Prior to the uprising these coffee plantations had become integral to the French economy and central to the expansion of French colonial power, including a demand for drugs and the slave labor that produced them. While most slaves in the Caribbean worked on sugar plantations, the major secondary crop was coffee, and France was not the only European power to benefit from the use of forced labor to produce increasingly desirable stimulants. European producers developed coffee plantations on Jamaica, St. Vincent, Grenada, St. Lucia, Trinidad, and Demerara (Guiana) (See Map 3.1). By the late eighteenth century, not only had European powers established coffee producing colonies throughout the Caribbean and along the coast of South America, they also relied on forced labor to produced coffee in the Indian Ocean colonies of Ceylon (today know as Sri Lanka), Java, Sumatra, Réunion, and Madagascar (See Map 3.2). While not the only reason for establishing colonies in these areas, the lucrative trade in coffee had a major impact on the decisions made by European authorities.

In British North America, the Virginia Colony produced the major share of tobacco for the world market by the late eighteenth century. After the American Revolution and the founding of the United States, Great Britain lost these major tobacco colonies. In order to sustain their share of the global tobacco market, British authorities established tobacco plantations in India. Earlier, in response to the production of British North American tobacco, Spain attempted to compete by establishing a royal tobacco monopoly in Cuba in 1717. The monopoly had the opposite effect and limited Cuban competition in the open market. Cuban tobacco farmers opposed the monopoly, and the Spanish government revoked it in June 1817 to take advantage of the British shift in production, allowing free trade between Cuba and the rest of the known world through Spanish ports. This move improved the position of Cuba in the global tobacco trade, which we will review later in the chapter. Also, sugar and rum production spread in the same colonies producing coffee, and by 1817 had become part of colonial production in Bengal, India.

At the outset of the nineteenth century European powers increased coffee production in certain areas of the world through the expansion of imperial holdings. A prime example of this in Britain's domination of Ceylon and the destruction of the Kingdom of Kandy. Elsewhere, after the Haitian Revolution (1791–1804) coffee production on the island decreased, thus opening up the potential for expansion in other locations. At that time, the other Caribbean islands were not in a position to increase production because of limitations of adequate

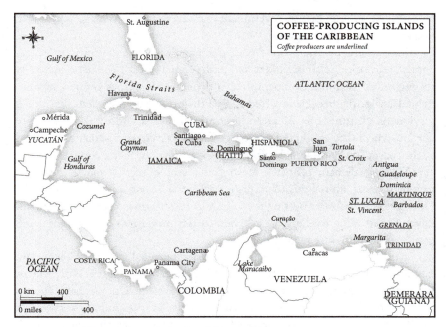

MAP 3.1 Coffee-Producing Islands of the Caribbean

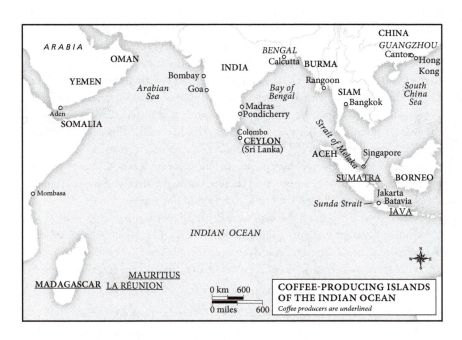

MAP 3.2 Coffee-Producing Islands of the Indian Ocean

land and labor.[4] The British government decided to take advantage of the void and increase their production.

This is where the connection between imperialism and coffee production becomes clear. Britain had been involved in the Indian Ocean coffee trade mainly through the East India Company, but in the early nineteenth century, governmental authorities became involved and set their sights on the island they called Ceylon. At the turn of the nineteenth century the Dutch controlled a portion of Ceylon, where they attempted to grow coffee. However, with influence confined to the coastal lowlands, Dutch efforts did not achieve any major commercial success. With the demand for coffee growing as a result of massive marketing, and a supply that was limited due to events in Haiti, the British moved to replace the Dutch in Ceylon. After ousting the Dutch in 1802, British agents found themselves in possession of the pearl fisheries, cotton plantations, salt, tobacco, and coffee production once held by the Dutch.[5]

To fully enlarge coffee production, the British needed to capture the mountainous highlands in the center of the island, then controlled by the independent Kingdom of Kandy. In order to claim the island for coffee production, Britain attacked the kingdom in a series of three wars between 1803 and 1815. However, the British needed an excuse for attacking the kingdom, which presented itself when officials of the Kandyan government attacked a group of Moorish (Islamic) British subjects conducting merchant activities with the kingdom. This led to a British force invading Kandyan lands on January 31, 1803. The *Times* of London supported the military actions while promoting support among the public, pushing the idea that the British did not want war, but that the Kingdom of Kandy was at fault. As the paper stated: "Every proposition to conciliate has been made to the Court of Candy [Kandy], and has been treated with disdain, which clearly proves the intention of that Court to avoid any reasonable arrangement."[6] The *Times* went on to argue that the Court of Kandy had initiated violence against the British, stating that "certain merchants, who had under the faith of treaties, purchased, at a fair market in the Candian [Kandyan] territories, Areka Nut, were despoiled of it forcibly by a person in authority under the Candian government."[7] British authorities portrayed themselves as the wronged party trying to do everything to avoid conflict, but Kandy would not agree.

British forces captured the capital and installed a puppet king, which was a common practice in British imperialism (See Figure 3-1). Despite Britain's overwhelming naval strength, Kandyan soldiers delivered heavy losses to British ground forces. Kandyan soldiers recaptured the capital city, installed King Sri

---

4. Bob Biderman, *A People's History of Coffee and Cafes* (Cambridge: Black Apollo Press, 2013), 117.

5. K. M. De Silva, *A History of Sri Lanka* (Berkeley: University of California Press, 1981), 225.

6. The *Times* (London), September 9, 1803, p. 3.

7. The *Times*, September 9, 1803, p. 3.

Vickrama Rajasinha back on the throne, and continued to fight the British for two more years until establishing a truce. Ever persistent, British authorities in Ceylon desired the entirety of the kingdom for increased coffee production. Since the war seemed to have been settled, and no longer being in possession of a pretext for attacking Kandy after the truce, Britain turned to another common tactic among imperial powers. In 1808, Britain supported a rebellion against Kandyan authority. Faced with internal disorder, King Rajasinha became more erratic in his rule, and the British used this to foment rebellion across the entire kingdom. By 1814 most of the population rebelled against the king, and the British used the rebellion as cover to invade again. In 1815, British agents worked with Kandyan nobility to remove the king and place the government under the ultimate control of the British governor in the military outpost of Colombo. At this point the press paid little attention to activities in Ceylon, as Britain gained the benefits of empire. One brief mention in the *Times* stated:

> It had been by a bloodless war on our side that the King of Kandy and his two wives have been made prisoner. But we are not able to pick out of the dispatches enough to qualify us to judge of the motives of these hostilities. The possession of a territory bountifully endowed with natural gifts would be but a moderate compensation, in a moral point of view, for the heavy guilt that would be incurred by undertaking an unjust or unprovoked war.[8]

FIGURE 3.1 "Town and Lake of Kandy'" by Charles O'Brien (1864).
Source: "Town and Lake of Kandy" by Charles O'Brien (1864)

---

8. The *Times* (London), August 4, 1815, p. 3.

The *Times* questioned the actions of British authorities using the Kandyan nobility, but nothing more was reported. The British then broke the power of the nobility, declared Colombo the new capital of Ceylon, and took complete control of the island by 1818.[9] By 1820, Great Britain started to establish major coffee plantations in the interior of the island.[10] The expansion of capitalist markets and commerce drove imperial actions in Ceylon, demonstrating the complete meshing of the two processes in spreading globalization.

Britain's geographic shift to the Indian Ocean roughly coincided with the abolition of the Atlantic slave trade within Britain's empire. Without free African labor at hand, British imperial authorities moved to reconstitute the slave system in order to intervene in the highly profitable coffee export markets enjoyed by its imperial rivals, France and the Netherlands. The production of coffee by African chattel slave labor in the Americas ended by the late nineteenth century, as slaves continued to rebel against the system and abolitionists forced the political issue. The plantation system using cheap labor continued to be profitable, so after the abolition of slavery Britain moved to reconstitute slavery by modified forms and by other names. Producers replaced African slaves with local labor in the colonies, continuing the exploitation and harsh treatment. On Ceylon, British plantation owners cleared much of the island's dense forest to make way for more coffee fields. Though the people of Ceylon produced their own coffee for local consumption, the new plantation system eliminated local independent production as British ownership quickly dominated the largest coffee plantations. By 1840, the British starting seizing "vacant" land for the crown in order to establish ever-larger estates to export tea and coffee.[11] What did the British mean by vacant land? They considered the land vacant if the natives living there were not using the land in a mode similar to that of the British plantation system.

To entice would-be plantation owners who were perhaps hesitant to put up the necessary capital for a large-scale Ceylon coffee venture, the British government provided land grants, tax exemptions, and relief from import duties for producers to cultivate coffee on the island.[12] Plantation owners colluded with imperial authorities to force local Tamil, an ethnic group indigenous to the island, to provide the bulk of the labor on the coffee plantations. But since

---

9. De Silva, *A History of Sri Lanka*, 226.

10. Rachel Kurian, "Labor, Race, and Gender on the Coffee Plantations in Ceylon," in *The Global Coffee Economy in Africa, Asia, and Latin America, 1500–1989*, ed. William G. Clarence-Smith and Steven Topik (Cambridge: Cambridge University Press, 2006), 173.

11. James S. Duncan, "Embodying Colonialism? Domination and Resistance in Nineteenth-Century Ceylonese Coffee Plantations," *Journal of Historical Geography* 28, no. 3 (2002): 320.

12. Kurian, "Labor, Race, and Gender," 174.

slavery was no longer legal within the empire, Britain needed another way of forcing Tamil onto plantations. The key was to eliminate the major source of Tamil income in the region: cotton cloth-weaving. Cheaper imports produced on vast scales in British factories increasingly powered by coal drove local Tamil producers out of business. When famine hit in 1837, many landless Tamil had no choice but to look for work in coffee and tea production. Deemed child-like, lazy, indolent, and sickly by British authorities, the Tamil—or "coolies," as the British callously called them—often fared little better than their African counterparts who worked the Caribbean plantations.[13] Though in theory free laborers, the experience of the Tamil in the British coffee fields of Ceylon demonstrated a great deal of continuity between the earlier drug production economies of the eighteenth-century Caribbean and new imperial plantations of the nineteenth century in the Indian Ocean. Coffee and empire had now foisted upon the inhabitants of Ceylon a global market-driven economy in which they had little say.

Another similar example of imperialism intertwining with industrial capitalism can be seen in the Dutch domination of Java. The Dutch collected coffee as taxes on their colony in West Java in the eighteenth century (explained in chapter 1), but after the demise of the Haitian coffee trade, the government decided to increase production in Java. In order to compete with the British, Governor-General Johannes van den Bosch's colonial government on Java forced native people to devote 20 percent of their land or labor to cultivating export crops, including coffee, to pay the colonial land tax to the Dutch government. We need to remember that coffee, while a main cash crop, was not the only one produced in this manner. Tobacco and indigo were also harvested under this cultivation system. The Dutch ran the coffee industry as a government monopoly with the native peoples forced to work the plantations. This system forced native populations to produce over 200 million pounds by the mid-nineteenth century.[14]

As we considered in chapter 1, the British colonies of Virginia and the Carolinas produced the majority of tobacco for the global market in the eighteenth century. After the founding of the United States, Great Britain lost control of these producing areas. The British government widened production in other colonies to compensate for the loss, with India becoming one area of increased production. The British East India Company started cultivation of American tobacco in India in the eighteenth century, so when the British government expanded

13. The term "coolies," while originating with the Tamil, became a common derogatory word for any unskilled worker in India, China, and the rest of Asia. James F. Hancock, *Plantation Crops, Plunder and Power: Evolution and Exploitation* (New York: Routledge, 2017), 148.

14. Hancock, *Plantation Crops, Plunder and Power*, 146.

their colonial presence in India, they grew tobacco production as well. Tobacco plantations under early nineteenth-century imperialism followed a similar plan as that of coffee plantations. The government took over so-called vacant land and forced native workers to serve on these plantations. Interestingly, the British shipped the cultivated tobacco to England and then imported smoking and chewing tobacco back into India for sale. Governments used this pattern with a variety of commodities, not just drugs, and it became a common pattern in modern globalization.

In the nineteenth century, Spain attempted to compete in the global tobacco market with Cuba becoming their main tobacco colony. The crown monopoly of tobacco ended in 1817, which regulated tobacco production to more local control. The crown monopoly is an example of an older style of imperial control, with the government dominating and controlling all aspects of production and sale. This form of control could not compete with the British style of allowing private merchants more jurisdiction and providing them access to land and workers through imperial domination. The lifting of the monopoly in Cuba allowed Cuban creoles[15] more control of the tobacco market, and the opportunity to operate their own plantations. The Spanish government hoped that lifting the monopoly would allow a more capitalist system, thereby increasing tobacco production. The change did increase tobacco production, and tobacco farms grew in number by 60 percent by 1862.[16] The government supported the new system and limited the freedom of the Cuban workers, keeping them on the tobacco and sugar plantations. The Spanish government also gave support in the form of tax breaks to the growing cigar industry. Spain promoted fine Cuban cigars on the global market as an exotic alternative to British and American tobacco. Governmental efforts made the Cuban cigar a favorite of the elites of the United States and Europe. The Spanish government changed their imperial policy in Cuba to compete on the global market, with an unforeseen side effect being the increase in ownership of tobacco farms and cigar factories by Cuban people of color in the nineteenth century. Cubans had more involvement in the global economy, which led them to resist Spanish imperial power more and more as the nineteenth century progressed.

As we mentioned in chapter 1, British colonialism, through the domination of the British navy, spread the rum trade on a global scale in the eighteenth century. The English started to produce rum in Bengal (a British colony in India) to ship to Australia.[17] A large portion of sugar production went into the distilling

---

15. Creoles in Cuba consisted of the descendants of Spanish immigrants to the island.

16. Charlotte A. Cosner, *The Golden Leaf: How Tobacco Shaped Cuba and the Atlantic World* (Nashville: Vanderbilt University Press, 2015), 138.

17. Geoffrey Blainey, *The Tyranny of Distance: How Distance Shaped Australia's History* (London: McMillian, 1966), 82.

of rum. In India, the British encouraged the large-scale production of sugar throughout the nineteenth century. Vast irrigation projects in northern India and lands that today are in Pakistan allowed more acreage to be turned over to sugar cane.[18] In their Indian holdings, the British forced the local people to produce the sugar for the global market, and due to low wages, poor conditions, and no control of the market, they were kept poor. The British then used a large portion of the sugar to distill rum with some Indian elites developing a taste for rum, increasing its demand. The British government supported McDowell and Company, a Scottish owned distiller, which became the foremost producer of rum in India. They shipped their product to Australia, New Zealand, and back to England.

While the British dominated India's rum market, they were not the only producers of the alcohol. The Dutch attempted to compete by producing rum in their colony in Batavia (today Jakarta, the capital of Indonesia). The Dutch enlarged their colony to cultivate sugar and produce rum, with the main brand being Batavia Arrack, distilled by E. & A. Scheer Company. The close relationship between government and private companies highlights the relationship of commerce and imperialism in early globalization. Batavia Arrack started to dominate the rum market across northern Europe. Asia was not the only region impacted by the rum trade and resulting imperialism. Rum also played a significant role in imperialism in Africa.

Just as in Asia, rum, slavery, and early imperialism in Africa were closely intertwined. By the eighteenth century a major part of the Atlantic slave trade consisted of selling rum in Africa and shipping slaves to the colonies in North and South America to produce sugar, tobacco, and coffee. The Oyo, Bornu, Dagbon, and Dahomey kingdoms of West Africa adopted rum as a major commodity, and the Portuguese, British, French, Dutch, and Danes built factories along the coast of Africa to trade rum and other goods, while shipping slaves to their colonies across the ocean. In the nineteenth century opposition started to limit the slave trade, but the demand for rum in Africa continued. European powers looked for new ways to use rum to dominate the various African societies and kingdoms.

The creation of Monrovia in today's Liberia exemplifies this strategy. Monrovia not only represents early United States imperialism, but it demonstrates how even after the colony achieved independence, it was still impacted by its legacy. In 1821, the American Colonization Society explored the idea of creating an African colony as a location to transplant freed slaves in the United States. The society obtained land at Cape Mesurado from the Dei and Bassa

---

18. Colonial India consisted of areas of what are today India, Pakistan, and Bangladesh. See also Charles A. Coulombe, *Rum* (New York: Citadel Press, 2004), 154.

people, using rum as the major payment for the location. Over 13,000 former slaves settled in the new colony (named after President James Monroe, who provided full government support), and the United States used rum to dominate Monrovia economically.[19] The colony stayed under the control of the United States until 1847, when the settlers declared it an independent republic. The Americo-Liberian settlers did not relate well to the indigenous population of the area, as they considered themselves superior and therefore thought they should be in control. The settlers attempted to dominate the area using rum as a major source of trade and political clout, since it still played a significant role in the local economy. This colony exemplified the tenets of imperialism that continued to play out in these colonies, as the Americo-Liberians using rum followed the colonial pattern already established.

In chapter 2 we explored the industrialization and commercialization of opium in the nineteenth century, referencing the colonization of India and other areas of Southeast Asia to produce opium for use in economic imperialism. In the early nineteenth century the British government relied on the East India Company (EIC) as the arm of its colonization. With British government approval, the EIC processed opium at factories in Patna and Benares to ship to China. The massive importation of opium to China offset the trade deficit Great Britain had with China, as explained earlier. The British government's use of opium to dominate China's economy was a form of economic imperialism, because Great Britain used the drug to improve their silver imbalance with China. The outflow of silver and the importation of opium, which caused economic difficulties in China, may not be the whole story. Some historians argue that the "balance of trade" theory of silver bullion outflow is inadequate in explaining the changes in silver in late imperial China, since opium accounts for only half the outflow of silver.[20] China was not a passive participant in the international market, and Chinese merchants traded silver because they could make a profit and bought commodities they lacked, which included opium.[21] However, from the British perspective opium provided the means to make a profit and acquire more silver. William Napier, as superintendent of British Trade, pushed for more British domination in China, increasing the sale of opium. Napier, a major imperialism supporter, believed that "might makes right" in the spread of capitalism and free trade.

---

19. For further research see James Ciment, *Another America: The Story of Liberia and the Former Slaves Who Ruled It* (New York: Hill and Wang, 2014) and C. Abayomi Cassell, *Liberia: History of the Frist African Republic* (New York: Fountainhead Publishers, 1970).

20. Frank Dikötter, Zhou Xun, and Lars Laamann, *Narcotic Culture: A History of Drugs in China* (London: Hurst & Company, 2004), 37.

21. Dikötter, Zhou, and Laamann, *Narcotic Culture*, 37.

In 1834 Chinese authorities attempted to restrict all British trade in response to Napier's actions, which led him to ordering British Royal warships to attack Chinese coastal forts. This imperialist action could have led to war, but Napier died of typhus, which halted the action. From the Chinese perspective, in addition to the decrease of silver, the growing opium addiction had a negative impact. By 1838 the number of Chinese opium addicts had grown to as many as twelve million, forcing the Chinese emperor to act. Opium addiction grew so rapidly that it began to affect the imperial troops and the official classes, which the emperor perceived as a major threat. Officials at the emperor's court disagreed about the proper policies the government should follow. Some officials advocated legalizing and taxing the trade in order to control it, while others advocated suppressing it. The faction wanting to ban opium completely won the debate by convincing the emperor of the grave threat to Chinese security. This decision and attempts by the Chinese government to stop the opium trade led to the Opium Wars, which represent a watershed moment in the spread of imperialism.

The New Imperialism

The Opium Wars represent a transition from early imperialism, where commercial interests dominated, to what some historians label the "new imperialism" in which imperial governments dominated the landscape, following the economic trends of the Industrial Revolution. At this point commerce, industrialization, and imperialism are completely intermeshed into a closed system, with the economies and societies of the colonies being controlled by the metropoles (the parent state of a colonial empire). The imperial governments fully supported private enterprise as a means to subjugate local economies and increase their own economic interests.

In 1839, in order to protect Chinese interests, the Daoguang Emperor appointed Lin Zexu, a scholar and official in his government, to the post of Special Imperial Commissioner to Canton, tasked with eradicating the opium trade.[22] The emperor made this decision after discovering that a close family member and several government officials had been caught smoking opium in one of the temples in the Forbidden Palace (the imperial palace in Beijing). This affront, and the fact that officials seized 130,000 ounces of opium in Tianjin, the main supply port of the capital, led the ruler to conclude that his earlier opium ban had failed. Lin's first act consisted of writing an open letter to Queen Victoria of England,

---

22. Lovell, *The Opium War*, 54.

appealing for an end to the trade.[23] Attempting to shame the British government, Lin questioned how Britain could be considered moral when its merchants profited from sales in China of a drug that caused such harm. He stated in the letter in 1839:

> Your Majesty has not before been thus officially notified, and you may plead ignorance of the severity of our laws, but I now give my assurance that we mean to cut this harmful drug forever.[24]

With the letter Lin tried to remove any chance that the queen and the British government could plead ignorance; however, the letter actually never reached the queen. Historians W. Travis Hanes and Frank Sanello suggest that it was lost in transit, but the fate of the letter is unknown.[25] Lin then banned the sale of opium in Canton and demanded that merchants surrender all supplies of the drug to Chinese authorities. He closed the Pearl River Channel, which trapped British traders in Canton, and seized thirteen opium factories in the city. As if this were not enough to increase friction between the two governments, he also ordered Chinese troops to board British ships in the Pearl River and South China Sea and destroy any opium on board. Charles Elliot, the British Superintendent of Trade in China (Napier's replacement), protested these actions, and ordered all ships carrying opium to flee as they prepared for battle. Elliot is considered by many historians to be the architect of Britain's Opium War with China.[26]

As we can see, Great Britain was creating a larger and more powerful empire over time. Historians have struggled to explain how the British Empire came to dominate a quarter of the world's land and population. Late nineteenth-century historians such as John Robert Seeley argued that the British Empire was accidental as a result of benign factors—Christian missionary work, attempts to better the world.[27] Seeley promoted the British Empire as a benevolent entity. Conversely, in the early twentieth century John Hobson, an English economist, argued that imperialism, characterized by economic exploitation, was the negative and unnecessary result of capitalist economies.[28] Hobson's

---

23. W. Travis Hanes III and Frank Sanello, *The Opium Wars: The Addiction of One Empire and the Corruption of Another* (Naperville, IL: Sourcebooks Inc., 2002), 39.

24. Lin Zexu, *Lin Zexu ji (Collected Works of Lin Zexu)* (Beijing: Zhonghua Shuju, 1962), 157.

25. Hanes, *The Opium Wars*, 41.

26. Lovell, *The Opium Wars*, 61.

27. See John Robert Seeley, *The Expansion of England* (Boston: Little, Brown & Co., 1883) and *The Growth of British Policy* (Cambridge: Cambridge University Press, 1896).

28. John A. Hobson, *Imperialism: A Study* (New York: James Pott & Co., 1902).

work would influence later scholars of imperialism. In the middle of the twentieth century, another school of thought influenced by John Gallagher and Ronald Robinson argued that European imperialism was a continuation of a long-term policy in which the formation of an informal empire, based on free trade, was favored over formal imperial control.[29] They stressed that imperialism is fully intertwined with economic expansion based on informal control. Early twenty-first-century Chinese historians' interpretations, specifically of the Opium Wars, assert that British imperialism consisted of a long-planned land and resources grab driven by greed.[30] Other theorists argued that the quest for military glory, safe sea routes, and new investment opportunities all played a role.[31] We also need to consider that British officials designed policy under pressure, in foreign environments via representatives without local competence working in isolation. As a result, the decisions being made by imperial powers were not always clear, planned, or coherent. So what is the correct interpretation? As we examine the events that occurred in the mid-nineteenth century, we can attempt to understand which interpretation (or aspects of several interpretations) best describe the actions of those involved. One central player in the events in China, Charles Elliot, personified imperialist ambition, opportunism, hypocrisy, and self-deception.[32]

Lin responded to Elliot's decision to continue the opium trade by holding foreign opium dealers in the foreign quarter of Canton, which kept them from communicating with their ships in port. Elliot decided to defuse the situation by convincing the British traders to cooperate with the Chinese and turn over their opium stockpiles. Elliot promised that their losses would be covered by the British government. Why is this promise made by Elliot important? Elliot made this promise on his own, but it obligated the British government to pay the cost of the lost private opium supplies. We can see from this example that at times imperial decisions were not clearly thought out. This promise amounted to a tacit acknowledgment that the British government did not disapprove of the trade, but more importantly, it placed a huge financial burden on the government. This promise—and the inability of the British government to pay for

29. John Gallagher and Ronald Robinson, "The Imperialism of Free Trade," *Economic History Review* 6, no. 1 (1953): 1–15.

30. See Lydia H. Liu, *The Clash of Empires: The Invention of China in Modern World-Making* (Cambridge, MA: Harvard University Press, 2004) and Man-houng Lin, *China Upside Down: Currency, Society, and Ideologies 1808–1856* (Cambridge, MA: Harvard University Press, 2007).

31. See Bernard Porter, *The Lion's Share: A History of British Imperialism 1850–2011* (Abingdon, UK: Routledge, 2012) and Raymond E. Dumett, *Gentlemanly Capitalism and British Imperialism: The New Debate on Empire* (Abingdon, UK: Routledge, 1999).

32. Lovell, *The Opium War*, 61.

it—was an important underlying cause for the subsequent British offensive. Elliot also knew that without opium Great Britain could slide into a deficit with China, this dilemma clearly showing the relationship between imperialism and industrial capitalism.

In April and May 1839, British and some American dealers surrendered 20,283 chests and 200 sacks of opium, which the Chinese destroyed.[33] After the British surrendered the opium, Lin allowed for other trade to continue in Canton. Lin announced that foreign merchants and Chinese officials must sign an agreement promising not to deal in opium under penalty of death. The British government opposed this agreement, as they felt it violated the principle of free trade, but some merchants (those not dealing in opium) signed the agreement against Elliot's orders. Regular trade continued but opium became scarce, which created a black market to meet high demand. Superintendent Elliot knew smugglers continued to import opium, but he turned a blind eye to the activities. The importance of this global trade to the economy of Great Britain is reflected in Elliot's decisions. Personally, he disliked opium and opium merchants; however, he believed that they were needed to sustain British domination in the Chinese market. Tensions continued to rise between the Chinese and the British. The build-up to the first Opium War provides insight into the imperialist mindset. British officials and merchants considered their economy, society, and desires superior to that of the Chinese. They justified their actions with the need and desire to strengthen and protect Great Britain. This attitude was not unique to the British, but the British example in China can provide us with a better understanding of the imperialist worldview and its interconnected relationship to industrial capitalism and the global market.

If we examine two events in the buildup to war, we can see the relationship between the imperialist mindset and global commerce. The first event, in July 1839, consisted of a group of British merchant sailors who, while drunk, killed a Chinese villager. Elliot arrested the men and refused to turn them over to Chinese authorities. He claimed that since the men were British, China had no authority over them. Elliot tried them himself and sentenced them to fines and hard labor, which British courts later overturned.[34] Lin stated that Great Britain had violated Chinese sovereignty and ordered that British ships could not purchase any supplies in China. The altercation all came to a head in Kowloon (part of today's Hong Kong), south of Canton. British ships attempted to purchase supplies from villagers in the region and Chinese military junks (sailing ships)

---

33. Lovell, *The Opium Wars*, 63.

34. Lovell, *The Opium Wars*, 94.

blocked them. Elliot ordered the British Royal Navy ships to fire on the Chinese vessels if they refused to move. The British drove off the Chinese ships in the Battle of Kowloon and purchased supplies from the villagers. Elliot used superior force to acquire supplies, stating:

> The men of the English nation desire nothing but peace; but they cannot submit to be poisoned and starved. The Imperial cruizers [warships] they have no wish to molest or impede; but they must not prevent the people from selling. To deprive men of food is the act only of the unfriendly and hostile.[35]

Elliot's statement blames the Chinese for getting in the way of the British. Elliot clearly believed that the British had the right of free trade with the Chinese, and that government rule must not hinder British commerce, especially for food.

The second event involved a brief struggle between private British merchants and British authority, which highlights the complexity of the relationship between imperialism and free trade. Several Quaker merchants disliked opium and refused to sell it, so they signed the Chinese agreement banning opium against Elliot's wishes. As a result, Lin allowed them to trade in Canton. Elliot—angered that they went against his orders—attempted to block these ships from traveling into Canton. The merchant ship *Royal Saxon* sailed past the blockade and the Royal navy ships fired warning shots at the merchant vessel. The Chinese sent junks to protect the *Royal Saxon*, and the British navy destroyed four Chinese junks. The British government, like other imperial governments, supported globalization and free trade, but only if it also supported their imperial designs.

After the Chinese crackdown on the opium trade, the British Parliament considered how to respond. A segment of the British population sympathized with Chinese desire to stop the sale of opium. However, Parliament and many British citizens expressed anger over the treatment of British diplomats and the protectionist trading policies of China. The Whig political party[36] controlled the government and advocated for war with China. The main issue that moved Britain toward war consisted of the interruption of free trade and commerce in China. In late 1839 reports published in London (pro-Whig) newspapers

---

35. *Correspondence Relating to China*, Presented to Both Houses of Parliament by Command of Her Majesty, 1840, accessed June 13, 2018, https://archive.org/details/CorrespondenceRelatingToChina1840/page/n4, 449.

36. The Whig party supported Parliament over the Monarchy and the expansion of free trade. The party had the full support of the wealthy merchants and industrial interests in Britain.

stressed the interference of trade and impending war. Parliament's Foreign Secretary Lord Palmerston, known for his aggressive foreign policy and as an advocate for free trade, believed that the destroyed opium was property, not contraband, and China must make reparations. He stated that no one could "say that he honestly believed the motive of the Chinese Government to have been the promotion of moral habits," arguing that the war was being fought to stem China's balance of payments deficit.[37] Palmerston pushed the Prime Minister William Melbourne for a military response, and with British merchants calling for an opening of free trade, the prime minister sent a force to China in October, 1839. British merchants argued that the Chinese consumers drove the opium trade; however, as we discovered in chapter 2, while this was part of the impetus, another major driving force was the producers and merchants themselves. The expulsion of British merchants from Canton and the refusal of the Chinese government to treat Britain as a diplomatic equal was also a slight to national pride.

Support for the war grew with the disruption of British trade and its impact on the British economy. This growing support for war reached as far as Queen Victoria, who on January 16, 1840, in her Annual Address to the House of Lords, expressed concerns over the interruption of commercial activities. These opinions demonstrate the connection between imperialism and globalization. While the opium trade sparked the conflict, the underlying issue was the spread of global trade. The increasing industrialization of Britain drove trade expansion globally, and the need for foreign markets and increased resources drove imperialism. The opium trade is an example of the interconnection between globalization, industrialization, and imperialism. In response to the queen's address, the Tories (the conservative opposition of the Whigs) attempted to gain more power in Parliament, accusing the Whigs of losing control over the foreign situation. Why was this opposition important? The opposition is important because it caused the Whigs to throw their support behind a war with China in order to strengthen their position. On July 27, 1840, the House of Commons finally agreed to grant funding for the war, long after the war had started. Great Britain, using their industrial might, defeated China, and the First Opium War officially ended on August 29, 1842, with the signing of the Treaty of Nanking (See Figure 3.2). The treaty represents a hallmark of British imperialism, with free trade and opium as a central point. The treaty opened up four more ports to British trade, and China paid for the destroyed opium. China also ceded Hong Kong to the British, and it became a crown colony. The treaty was later

---

37. Glenn Melancon, *Britain's China Policy and the Opium Crisis: Balancing Drugs, Violence and National Honour, 1833–1840* (London: Ashgate, 2003), 126.

FIGURE 3.2 The East India Company iron steam ship Nemesis destroying Chinese war junks in Anson's Bay, on January 7, 1841. The image demonstrates the close connection between the British government and opium merchants during the First Opium War. Edward Duncan, 1841.

Source: Edward Duncan/Wikipedia, https://commons.wikimedia.org/wiki/File:Destroying_Chinese_war_junks,_by_E._Duncan_(1843).jpg

supplemented with the Treaty of the Bogue, which recognized Britain as an equal to China and exempted British subjects from local law in treaty ports. At the end of the First Opium War, Great Britain still imported opium and now dominated the Chinese economy even more.

As we move into the 1850s, Western imperialism spread rapidly. As production of commodities increased due to the demands of the Industrial Revolution, Western powers developed their overseas markets and established new ports to sell goods. Globalization increased the spread of Western political and economic domination and control. The British put more pressure on the Chinese government, demanding that China open all of the country to British merchant companies and legalize the opium trade. Britain also wanted foreign imports exempted from internal transit duties, and all treaties between the governments to be in English, not Chinese.[38] The Qing government weakened under British imperialism and the Second Opium War soon broke out

---

38. Hanes, *The Opium Wars*, 164.

due to the tensions between the two governments. Because of a weakening Chinese government and economy, the Taiping Rebellion broke out in 1851.[39] While the rebellion was not directly part of the Second Opium War, it did provide the backdrop for conditions in China as the waning economy led to the rebellion. The rebellion consisted of a combination of military action, religious-political repression and retaliation, and a resulting famine that claimed the lives of between twenty and thirty million people.[40] The rebellion, which ended in 1864, weakened the Qing government but also threatened the British holdings, as the rebels seized large portions of land and disrupted the Chinese economy, thereby impacting British trade. We will not review the Taiping rebellion in detail in this volume, but it is important to note that several complex events all played a role in the relationship between imperialism and global trade.

The Second Opium War began in 1856, with the Chinese seizing the cargo ship the *Arrow*. The British treated Chinese merchant vessels that operated in their Chinese treaty ports the same as British ships. British authorities granted these vessels British registration in Hong Kong, illustrating British domination of these ports and the merchant economy. In October 1856, Chinese authorities seized the *Arrow* in Canton on suspicion of piracy. The ship, a former pirate vessel, was registered with the British. The authorities arrested the crew and pulled down the British flag, which Britain considered a major insult, demanding an apology and the release of the crew. This did not happen in a manner that appeased the British, and as a result they attacked four Chinese coastal forts and launched an attack that captured Canton. As we can see from this incident, an imperial power could use the slightest insult to their sovereignty as an excuse to dominate other areas. France, Russia, and the United States all pledged aid to the British to subjugate China. The three nations wanted to become involved to increase their own economic power in the country. Using imperialist actions as a means to increase global economic power and markets was not limited to the British.

The war lasted until October 18, 1860, with the ratification of the Treaty of Tianjin. The Chinese government did not have the military power to fight the Taiping Rebellion and the Western powers. The end of the war and the treaty clearly established the imperial domination of the West. The Chinese had to pay for the cost of the war, and Britain acquired Kowloon (next to Hong

---

39. For more research on the Taiping Rebellion see Shunshin Chin and Joshua A. Fogel, *The Taiping Rebellion* (Armonk, NY: M. E. Sharpe, 2001) and Daye Zhang and Xiaofei Tian, *The World of a Tiny Insect: A Memoir of the Taiping Rebellion and Its Aftermath* (Seattle: University of Washington Press, 2014).

40. Hanes, *The Opium War*, 167.

Kong). The treaty legalized the opium trade and Christians were granted full civil rights, which increased Christian missionary activities. Another aspect of the treaty allowed the British to transport indentured Chinese workers to work in other British colonies, mostly in the Americas. The two opium wars not only increased British dominion over China, but signify a shift to a larger and more encompassing form of imperialism. What some historians have called the new imperialism began in the 1860s and 1870s. The drive behind this amplified imperialism—the demands of the Industrial Revolution and monopoly capitalism—moved the imperialist Western powers to seek a monopoly over resources and markets around the world, and thereby increase the globalization of drugs.

The Role of New Imperialism in the Growth of the Drug Market

New imperialism characterizes a period of colonial expansion by European powers, as well as the United States and Japan, during the late nineteenth and early twentieth centuries. During this period, imperial powers pursued overseas territorial acquisitions more than ever before. Imperial states focused on building their empires with new technological advances and developments brought to them by the Industrial Revolution. They increased their territories through conquest, while exploiting the resources of the subjugated countries. During the era of new imperialism, the imperial powers individually conquered almost all of Africa and large parts of Asia. The new wave of imperialism also reflected ongoing competition between the great powers, driven by the economic greed for new resources and markets. Many of the imperial powers' major elites found advantages in formal, overseas expansion, as large financial and industrial monopolies sought imperial support to protect their overseas investments against competition and domestic political tensions abroad. Special interests perpetuated empire-building, as bureaucrats sought government offices, military officers looked for promotion, and traditional but fading landed gentries sought increased profits for their investments. The increase in imperialism, driven by industrial capitalism, swelled drug production in the colonies and increased the market globally. This can be illustrated by the role of opium and cocaine in the globalization of imperial markets.

After the Opium Wars in China the Chinese government lacked the political power to stop the opium trade, and the British government in the late nineteenth century had no desire to end the trade while they were making a fortune from the drug. It is important we understand that the role opium played in China was not just about addiction. Opium provided economic gain; it took on the role of a status symbol, and it allowed workers and the elite a means for relaxation and recreation.[41] The choices of Chinese consumers played a major role. Since the Treaty of Tianjin legalized the opium trade, Britain started to shift production of opium from India to China in order to save on transportation costs. This shift initiated massive domestic production, and importation of opium from India peaked in 1879 at 6,700 tons per year. After this point, domestic production in China dominated the trade and importation from India continued to decrease. By the 1880s, even governors who had initially suppressed opium smoking and poppy production now depended on opium taxes. In the stagnating Chinese economy opium supplied fluid capital and created new sources of taxes. Smugglers, poor farmers, coolies, retail merchants, and officials all depended on opium for their livelihood. Opium production multiplied and by 1906 China was producing 85 percent of the world's opium, some 35,000 tons.

The opium trade saw a major readjustment in the second half of the nineteenth century. Not only did legalization give impetus to Chinese domestic production, but it also made the trade seem Asian and not European.[42] British and other European opium traders used opium to move into and dominate the Asian market, but after opium production moved to China, they faded out of the trade and passed the market into the hands of locally based Asian traders. Because of imperialism, opium was also part of a fully global market. Britain still made money from the trade, but in India, Parsi, Armenian, Jewish, and Muslim firms started playing an important role, and being seen as white or British no longer gave the trader the same competitive advantage.[43] The firms now moving the drugs were part of the colonial empire.

For example, the British company Jardine Matheson of Hong Kong and its associate company Jardine Skinner & Co of Calcutta established a dominant position in the opium trade by 1860. The company formed the Malwa Opium Syndicate controlling a major portion of the trade out of Malwa (a region in north-central India). The syndicate produced opium in Malwa for shipment to China and other parts of Asia for over thirty years.[44] After production moved to China, Jardine Matheson left the opium trade behind and used their position to profit from other global markets, moving into tea, silk, insurance, and banking. They would be replaced by David Sassoon & Company, producing opium in China using Chinese labor. David Sassoon belonged to a Jewish trading family established in Persia, which moved to China

41. Dikötter et al., *Narcotic Culture*, 48–50.

42. Carl A. Trocki, *Opium, Empire and the Global Political Economy* (London: Routledge, 1999), 109.

43. Trocki, *Opium, Empire and the Global Political Economy*, 109.

44. Trocki, *Opium, Empire and the Global Political Economy*, 112.

in 1871, becoming a leader in the Asian opium trade. This transition high-lights the globalization of the drug and the role of the British colonial empire. The British Empire made it easier for a globalized market to develop, and Britain did not care who produced the drug as long as they made money off the market. As opium production moved from India to China, local Chinese guilds had more influence over the production process. However, Britain still controlled the distribution network, which allowed them to ultimately con-trol the trade.

Cocaine also offers an example of a different form of imperialism—economic imperialism. Peru became independent in 1824, but the new country needed to establish a stable economy. At first these efforts were successful, but by 1870 the Peruvian economy was suffering. This allowed heavy foreign investment to domi-nate the resources of the new nation. In the decades after 1860, some Peruvian pharmacists, medical authorities, promoters, and statesmen began recasting the possibilities of the coca leaf and cocaine in order to stimulate the economy. The development of the Peruvian cocaine market yields insight into the complexi-ties of economic imperialism and lays the foundation for the subsequent war on drugs of the twentieth century (see chapter 5).

Companies in the United States and Germany drove the global cocaine market of the nineteenth century with involvement of local producers. American and German companies were central to the industrialization and commercialization of cocaine in the nineteenth century, which we considered in chapter 2. This is only part of the story, as these companies needed to ensure a continuous supply of coca leaves or raw cocaine. The drug manufacturers invested heavily in the economy of Peru, and many petty industrialists and colonizing planters relied on this investment.[45] If we look closer at the co-caine industry and economic imperialism in Peru, we can see that the Peruvian government and local elites were closely enmeshed with and dependent on the foreign investment. In the 1890s Peru became the unrivaled producer of raw cocaine, supplying the tons needed for the global appetites for the drug. This structured local regional economies based on cocaine and inspired na-tional identification with the drug.[46] Economic imperialism developed the local Peruvian cocaine industry, but the ultimate control of drug was held by foreign (US) interests. By 1900 the United States was the world's major consumer of cocaine, mainly through patent medicines and soft drinks. By 1900 the United States also produced a third of the world's cocaine, using Peruvian coca and raw cocaine. Coca production became a significant part of

---

45. Paul Gootenberg, *Andean Cocaine: The Making of a Global Drug* (Chapel Hill: University of North Carolina Press, 2008), 56.

46. Gootenberg, *Andean Cocaine*, 56.

the economy of Peru, which was completely entangled with and dominated by United States industry and commerce. We will explore this relationship in more depth in chapter 5.

The changes in the world economy through globalization and expansion of imperialism becomes more complex regarding coffee, tobacco, and rum. Imperial powers using economic imperialism took the lead with coffee and tobacco, especially in the new nations of Central and South America. Coffee production continued in Java and Ceylon, but suffered due to leaf blight after 1870. Imperial powers then developed new areas of coffee production in the Philippines and Hawaii. Major expansion focused on Latin America, with foreign companies and investment dominating production. Coffee production in Brazil exemplifies these changes and the growing complexity of the global market. Brazil became independent from Portugal in 1825 as a monarchy, until 1894, when a republic was established. After independence Brazil establish a thriving coffee industry, producing 70 percent of the world's coffee by the 1890s. A wealthy landed class dominated the coffee industry, with a small group of landowners controlling most of the coffee-producing land.[47] These landowners and the economy of Brazil became dependent on foreign (mostly US) support and investment. Coffee became the main export, with little production in other areas, forcing Brazil to import most other products. This system created a booming economy that was unstable and dependent on foreign companies. This illustrates the complexity of economic imperialism, as the economy of Brazil seemed to be expanding, but only a small portion of the population benefited from the wealth. Another aspect of coffee production in Brazil was the globalization of labor. Brazil abolished slavery in 1888, which left them a labor shortage for coffee production. At first Italian immigrants moved to the country to work on coffee plantations, but poor treatment resulted in Italy enacting legislation prohibiting subsidized immigration to Brazil.[48] To help with the labor shortage, Brazil allowed immigration from Japan in 1908, with large numbers of Japanese immigrants entering to work on coffee plantations.

Tobacco continued to be grown in the United States, China, India, Cuba, and other regions of Latin America, with few changes except an increase in production. The development of a cigarette-making machine in the 1880s increased the availability of cigarettes, which in turn increased demand. Cuban cigars

---

47. Hildete Perira de Melo, "Coffee and Development of the Rio de Janeiro Economy 1888–1920," in *The Global Coffee Economy in Africa, Asia, and Latin America, 1500–1989*, ed. William Gervase Clarence-Smith and Steven Toki (Cambridge: Cambridge University Press, 2003), 371.

48. Bob Biderman, *A People's History of Coffee and Cafes* (Cambridge: Black Apollo Press, 2013), 227.

continued to be produced, but after the Spanish–American War in 1898, the island would be subjugated by the United States even after formal independence in 1902. The United States supervised Cuban finance, and American businesses controlled the island, developing a form of American imperialism. Rum continued to be used as an instrument of imperialism in Africa in the late nineteenth and early twentieth century. Imperial powers used the rum trade as a way to establish economic control and provide easy access to the product, which made the intoxicated easy to control. This was the case in Nigeria, South Africa, Angola, and the Belgian Congo.

Attitudes toward opium started to shift in the late nineteenth century. In the 1890s, Protestant missionaries in China decided to voice their opposition to the opium trade by compiling data that demonstrated the drug's harm and arousing public opinion against the trade. Missionaries faced an image problem: the Chinese linked Christianity to opium, since the early missionaries came over on opium ships. To overcome this issue, in 1890, at the Shanghai Missionary Conference, anti-opium missionaries established the Permanent Committee for the Promotion of Anti-Opium Societies.[49] Pressure from missionary societies caused the British government to create the Royal Commission on Opium in 1893, which scrutinized the opium trade from India to China to determine if the trade should be stopped.[50] Members of the commission visited India in 1895, reporting that opium was not harmful to the Chinese and that it was no different than alcohol. The commission report argued that the issue was not that of health or addiction but instead a commercial complaint, which would decrease as production moved from India to China. Anti-opium societies were outraged because the commissioners only visited India, and never went to China to examine the situation there. It is clear that the government in Great Britain found the trade too valuable to end.

By 1906 the importance of the Western opium trade with China had declined, and the Qing government was able to begin to regulate the importation and consumption of the drug. In 1907 China signed the Ten Years' Agreement with India, whereby China agreed to forbid native cultivation and consumption of opium on the understanding that the export of Indian opium would decline in proportion and cease completely in 10 years. The trade thus almost completely stopped by 1917. Opium smoking and addiction remained a problem in China in subsequent decades, since the weakened central government could not wipe out the native cultivation of opium.

---

49. Virginia Berridge, *Demons: Our Changing Attitudes to Alcohol, Tobacco, and Drugs* (New York: Oxford University Press, 2013), 184.

50. Berridge, *Demons,* 186.

Globalization could not have spread as quickly as it did without the advent of imperialism. As we have seen, industrial capitalism and imperialism are two sides of the same coin, both driving globalization. As we move into the early twentieth century, there was a shift in attitude toward the global use and trade of certain drugs. The idea that the trade and use of these drugs should be limited, if not fully prohibited, gained traction due to the social cost. In the next chapter we will examine this shift toward the prohibition of opium, cocaine, and rum (as well as other alcohol), while coffee and tobacco continued to thrive.

FURTHER READING

Feiling, Tom. *Cocaine Nation: How the White Trade Took over the World*. New York: Pegasus Books, 2012.

Kessler, Lawrence. "A Plantation Upon a Hill; Or, Sugar without Rum: Hawai'i's Missionaries and the Founding of the Sugarcane Plantation System." *Pacific Historical Review* 84, no. 2 (2015): 129–62.

Lovell, Julia. *The Opium War: Drugs, Dreams and the Making of Modern China*. New York: Overlook Press, 2015.

Mills, James. *Drugs and Empires: Essays in Modern Imperialism and Intoxication, c. 1500–c. 1930*. London: Palgrave Macmillan, 2007.

Richards, John. "Opium and the British Indian Empire: The Royal Commission of 1895." *Modern Asian Studies* 36, no. 2 (2002): 375–420.

4

PROHIBITION AND THE CIVILIZING MISSION

On June 7, 1900, Carrie A. Nation gathered several rocks, which she called "smashers," and proceeded to Dobson's Saloon in Kiowa, Kansas, where she used the rocks to destroy the saloon's stock of alcohol.[1] Nation, a member of the American temperance movement and founder of the Medicine Lodge, Kansas chapter of the Women's Christian Temperance Union, strongly believed that the Christian God had commanded her to destroy liquor establishments (See Figure 4.1). As she stated in her autobiography, He instructed her to "take something in your hands and throw at these places in Kiowa and smash them."[2] After she destroyed two more saloons in Kiowa, a tornado hit eastern Kansas, which she saw as divine approval of her actions.

Temperance, a social movement against the consumption of alcohol, first emerged in Great Britain and the United States in the 1820s in response to the increased production and use of alcohol, and the attendant perceived social problems. Nation joined the movement after her first husband became a heavy drinker. She continued destroying saloons in Kansas, her fame only increasing as her arrest record spiked. After leading a raid in Wichita, Nation started using a hatchet after her second husband joked that she needed to inflict maximum damage. Between 1900 and 1910, Nation was arrested over 30 times for "hatchetations," as she called her attacks. Nation paid her jail fines from lecture tour fees and sales of souvenir hatchets with "Death to Rum" engraved on the handle.[3] As she gained fame, she moved to attack the Senate Bar in the state's capital of Topeka. The bar was the favorite of state officials, and on February 5, 1901, she destroyed the establishment. As she later wrote:

> I ran behind the bar, smashed the mirror and all the bottles under it; picked up the cash register, threw it down; then broke

---

1. Frances Grace Carver, "With Bible in One Hand and Battle-Axe in the Other: Carry A. Nation as Religious Performer and Self-Promoter," *Religion and American Culture: A Journal of Interpretation* 9, no. 1 (1999): 37.

2. Carry A. Nation, *The Uses and Need of the Life of Carry A. Nation* (Topeka, KS: F. M. Steves, 1905), 130.

3. Daniel Okrent, *Last Call: The Rise and Fall of Prohibition* (New York: Scribner, 2010), 29.

FIGURE 4.1 Carrie Nation with her bible and her hatchet. Nation represents the passion and superior attitude behind the civilizing mission.
Source: Heritage Image Partnership Ltd/Alamy Stock Photo

the faucets of the refrigerator, opened the door and cut the rubber tubes that conducted the beer. Of course, it began to fly over the house. I threw over the slot machine, breaking it up and I got from it a sharp piece of iron with which I opened the bungs of the beer kegs, and opened the faucets of the barrels, and then beer flew in every direction and I was completely saturated. A policeman came in and very good-naturedly arrested me.[4]

Carrie Nation's aggressive campaign, while seemingly geographically isolated and focused on alcohol, is instructive of important shifts in the global drug trade at the turn of the twentieth century. In chapter 2, we examined how industrialization drove globalization by transforming the production and nature of drugs in Europe and America during the Industrial Revolution. In chapter 3, we examined how Western imperialism intensified globalization during the nineteenth century by forcibly integrating far-flung resources, markets, and populations into larger economic and political structures, a central feature of which was monopoly

4. Nation, *Uses and Need*, 166.

capitalism. By the end of the nineteenth century most regions of the world had become part of a globalized market for alcohol and other drugs.

Western moral reformers like Nation seldom tried to stop or even question these imperial projects, which almost always carried with them the production, circulation, and distribution of drugs. They instead worked to reform existing empires they believed to be engaged in excess. The increased mass consumption of drugs due to industrial production, commercialization, and imperialism had in fact produced heavy social costs. While coffee and tobacco (chapter 1) elicited minimal critique, alcohol, opium, and cocaine became the focus of a set of global efforts to stamp out what reformers saw as a key negative impact of globalization.

Nation and others believed that only Western Christian morals could halt the destructive impacts of the international trade in alcohol, opium, and cocaine at both local and global levels. Nation believed herself to be a "instrument of God" and a "watchdog of Jesus" with the goal of reform in not only the United States, but in the wider world.[5] While Nation mainly operated in Kansas and Oklahoma, she and her fellow reformers imagined their efforts as part of a global mission aimed at curbing the trade and consumption of drugs. In this sense, temperance and prohibition advocates fought against the currents of globalization that helped to create international markets for drugs in the first place. Yet these reformers also benefitted from the speed and scale of travel and communication that globalization afforded to bring their message to those they believed most needed it.[6]

During the Age of Empire (1870–1914), Europeans, together with Euro-Americans, conceived of themselves as engaged in a "civilizing mission" designed to impart Western culture, thoughts, education, language, science, logic, and morality to colonized non-Europeans. Imperialists thought that it was the duty of the supposedly morally superior Western nations to educate and civilize the indigenous people in the colonies to protect them from dangerous influences. Anti-drug activists supported the civilizing mission by arguing that non-Western people of the world needed protection from vice and temptation because they lacked the moral fortitude to do so on their own. Western reformers rarely resisted the spread of this type of paternalistic imperialism. Instead, they actively encouraged it.

As such, by the turn of the twentieth century, tensions between the economic and political interests promoting the global distribution of drugs and Protestant moralists who wished to limit or prohibit certain drugs came to a head over the civilizing mission. Would empire protect, in however paternalistic a fashion, non-white colonial subjects? Or would economics further contribute to their misery?

---

5. Carver, "With Bible in One Hand," 40.

6. Heather Streets-Salter and Trevor Getz, *Empires and the Colonies in the Modern World: A Global Perspective* (New York: Oxford University Press, 2016), 8.

To demonstrate the tension, which was never fully resolved, this chapter focuses on the impact of reformers in Britain and the United States, imperial powers heavily involved in the international drug trade. But citizens and officials in both nations also participated heavily in cultural imperialism. Anglo-American Protestant reformers became central to promoting the civilizing mission. They believed that colonized subjects, including native people in the American and Canadian west, required education, uplift, and protection from the worst excesses of empire. Only the superior morality of white Britons and Americans, these reformers argued, could accomplish this goal. What they accomplished instead was the unintended creation of black markets where the drug trade continued to thrive. Attempting to reign in the power of global capitalism, these reformers found, was as difficult a task as convincing colonial subjects that they needed to conform to Anglo-American norms.

Demon Rum: Temperance and the Failure of Prohibition

The Anglo-American push to reform and civilize the world drove the temperance movement on local and global levels. In the United States the movement began at a national level in the early 1820s, among middle-class Protestant evangelical reformers.[7] The earliest temperance advocates concentrated at first on hard spirits rather than on abstinence from all alcohol, as they saw the stronger liquors a greater moral threat. In the 1820s and 1830s the movement gained more supporters as the Second Great Awakening, an Evangelical Protestant religious revival, promoted a more Christian society. Many Evangelical Protestants believed that they needed to make the world a better place and remedy the evils of society wrought by globalization and industrialization.

While temperance became a widespread social movement and nonsectarian in principle, it consisted mostly of Protestant church members. These early movements, focusing on national reform, emphasized the moral, economical, and medical effects of overindulgence with a strong connection to formal religious organizations. Alcohol producers and merchants had already created a powerful global market fully intertwined in the economies of many Western nations. Still, the temperance movement grew as reformers saw it as the Christian duty to civilize society. Anglo-American reformers determined that they needed to not only work in their own nations, but to reform other areas of the world as well. The 1830s then saw a tremendous growth in temperance groups not only in England

---

7. Katherine Chavigny, "Reforming Drunkards in Nineteenth-Century America: Religion, Medicine, Therapy," in *Altering American Consciousness: The History of Alcohol and Drug Use in the United States, 1800–2000,* ed. Sarah W. Tracy and Caroline Jean Acker (Amherst: University of Massachusetts Press, 2004), 109.

and the United States, but in some of Britain's white settler colonies, especially New Zealand and Australia.

Unsurprisingly, alcohol manufacturers saw these movements as threats to profits, and they worked to promote drinking as a normal social exercise. Despite these attempts to counter the anti-alcohol craze, the movement continued to grow. However, not all citizens supported temperance. Considering drinking an important part of their cultures, German and Irish immigrants to the United States resisted the movement. Alcohol manufacturers often targeted these groups with massive advertising campaigns.

Activists in the United States and the United Kingdom dominated the temperance movement of the nineteenth century, since the foundation of the movement resided in Evangelical Protestant beliefs like those of the Second Great Awakening. The movement gained little traction in Germany and Denmark as anti-globalization individualistic Anglo-American ideas had a lesser impact. Similarly, few European Catholics or Jews joined the movements. Many Europeans in general considered the consumption of wine or beer an integral part of daily life. Total prohibition, they argued, went too far.[8]

Elsewhere in the world, Muslims, Buddhists, and Hindus resisted temperance movements. These three religions promoted abstinence, practitioners believing abstaining should be a religious choice and not a government compulsion, especially when the government compulsion consisted of imperial dominance. These religious practitioners also resisted the Christian domination of the movement. Those areas under the domination or influence of the Western imperial powers would be the target of Western reformers' desire to civilize the empire by trying to instill Christian values. Later in the second half of the twentieth century, after India and other countries had won independence, some of the new governments of these areas would enact prohibition laws to limit Western globalized influences.

In Britain, reformers extended the colonial civilizing mission to working-class Britons as well. The upper and middle classes saw the industrial working class as susceptible to degenerate behavior and thought they needed to be saved from their own impulses. For example, the Band of Hope, founded in 1847 in Leeds, England, worked to allegedly rescue working-class children from their drinking parents by teaching them the importance and principles of sobriety and abstinence.[9] Meetings held in churches throughout the United Kingdom included Christian instruction, and the group campaigned politically against the influence

---

8. Ian Tyrrell, *Woman's World Women's Empire: The Women's Christian Temperance Union in International Perspective, 1880–1930* (Chapel Hill: University of North Carolina Press, 1991), 66–67.

9. Re H. Marles, *The Life and Labours of the Rev. Jabez Tunnicliff* (London: William Tweedle, 1865), 213.

of public house owners and brewers. The organization—considered radical for its time—organized rallies, demonstrations, and marches to influence people to sign an alcohol abstinence pledge. The reformers felt the need to civilize their own citizens, but that represented only a small part of what was needed.

One major example is the Woman's Christian Temperance Union (WCTU), formed in the United States in 1873, which represented a group that started nationally but quickly moved to spread Anglo-American reform in colonies and on continental frontiers. Women formed the base and major force of the temperance movement because they believed alcohol disproportionately threatened women and children. In keeping with nineteenth-century Victorian notions of how families were supposed to operate, they saw that drunken heads of household (men) threatened the entire social and moral stability of the family unit. This argument extended far beyond white working- and middle-class American and British families, to nonwhites in the colonies and within the United States.

Despite its origins among Protestant organizations, the United States government itself attempted to limit access to alcohol on Indian reservations. Beginning in the 1870s, US officials and social reformers campaigned to assimilate Native Americans into "American" culture, a process that involved boarding schools, child separation policies, and claims of the inevitable demise of American Indians if they did not conform to modern industrial and agricultural life. Prohibition fit rather neatly into this plan. Few US officials saw the hypocrisy in demanding assimilation of Indians and claims that they could not handle assimilation. They argued that it was necessary to civilize native peoples by removing alcohol since they did not have the moral fortitude to resist temptation on their own. Assimilation under the watchful eye of Protestant mother and father figures became the social norm.[10]

Members of the WCTU took up the campaign in 1879 when Mary Lucinda Bonney began to call attention to the plight of Native Americans. Influenced by the social activism and reform ideas that formed out of the Second Great Awakening, Bonney felt that church organizations had so far failed to reform American Indians, particularly native women. Bonney approached her close friend Amelia Strong Quinton, a member of the WCTU. The two formed the Women's National Indian Association (WNIA) to "save" Native Americans living in squalid conditions in Indian territory.[11] The new organization focused on women and children and the problem of alcohol on reservations. The underlying philosophy of the WNIA rested on the belief that non-Christian women

---

10. William Unrau, *White Man's Wicked Water: The Alcohol Trade and Prohibition in Indian Country 1802–1892* (Lawrence: University of Kansas Press, 1996), 115.

11. Valerie Sherer Mathes, "Nineteenth Century Women and Reform: The Women's National Indian Association," *American Indian Quarterly* 14, no. 1 (Winter 1990): 2–3.

lived degraded lives. Bonney and Quinton saw Indians as child-like, hedonistic, and in dire need of proper cleansing. The solution? Eradicate native culture and replace it with one rooted in white American norms. But WNIA members also recognized that the problem of alcohol had not originated on reservations but had arrived with the westward expansion of white settlers. Therefore, the WNIA saw the reform of the internally colonized (American Indians) and the colonizer (white male settlers) as twinned projects.[12]

The WCTU, the WNIA's parent organization, started directly working in Indian territory (present-day Oklahoma) in the early 1880s. WCTU organizers believed that lawlessness and disorder among native peoples resulted from excess liquor. The stereotype of the "drunken Indian" had become part of American popular culture earlier in the century, and this stereotype conditioned reformers to believe that native communities especially needed their help.[13] This paternalistic attitude was a major part of internal American imperialism. Frances Willard, president of the WTCU, visited Indian territory in 1881 to spread the temperance message. Jane Stapler, a prominent Cherokee woman, along with several others, formed a welcoming committee to make Willard's visit comfortable.[14] Willard, amazed at the prosperity of Tahlequah, the capital of the Cherokee Nation, decided that the Cherokee represented a powerful partner for the WCTU. She recruited Jane Stapler as the head of the Tahlequah chapter, and temperance gained ground among the Cherokee. Willard considered the Cherokee a good example of assimilation into American culture, with native reformers in the vanguard to stop the spread of alcohol in Indian territory.

The WCTU gained influence in Indian territory because of the work of Jane Stapler and other Native women who joined the movement. Interactions of the WCTU led the reformers to develop a better opinion of Native Americans; however, the WCTU would take all the credit. When Barbara O'Brian, a WCTU organizer, visited Stapler in 1889, she commented on the orderly and organized proceedings. She did not give credit to the Cherokee, but stated that it was caused by the civilizing influence of the WCTU.[15] These white women believed that their cultural superiority was the deciding factor.

With its teeth cut in Indian territory, the WCTU began to look beyond the frontier and US borders by the 1880s. Leadership argued that only a full-fledged international assault on alcohol could stop its flow both at home and abroad. Their outlook was decidedly international in this sense. But it also dripped with notions

---

12. Mathes, "Nineteenth Century Women," 2.

13. Izumi Ishii, "Not a Wigwam Nor Blanket Nor Warwhoop: Cherokees and the Women's Christian Temperance Union," *Journal of American and Canadian Studies* 18 (2000): 3.

14. Ishii, "Not a Wigwam," 4.

15. Ishii, "Not a Wigwam," 10.

of Anglo-American racial and cultural superiority as the only possible solution to drunkenness among nonwhites living in formal and informal colonies. These communities lacked the racial fortitude to even identify, much less solve, the problem on their own, such arguments went, which led Frances Willard to found the World Woman's Christian Temperance Union (WWCTU) in 1883.[16] The WWCTU used Willard's policies and extended its influence beyond its own ranks to include many other church people, including men. The WCTU could then operate on an international scale with an interlocking set of organizations and individuals creating a constituency of Anglo-American internationalism across North Africa and Asia.

While other temperance organizations existed in Britain and some of its colonies, the American movement that created the WCTU surpassed them.[17] Willard and other WCTU activists toured North Africa, the Middle East, China, and Japan. While their promotion of the United States as moral leader was intended to spur American activists at home, it also spurred the creation of a more international movement. Mary Clement Leavitt, whom Willard sent on a globe-circling missionary trip to advance the work of the WWCTU, stressed the superiority of Americans in the matter of drinking patterns. She stated, "America should see that she is the Messiah of the nations; that she is to give other nations better than they ever dreamed of." We can see by this quote that the movement pushed a religious Anglo-American agenda internationally. This push of American (read: Protestant) morality on an international level represented US cultural imperialism and the globalization of American moral ideas to its logical extreme.

An example of this can be seen in the WWCTU activism in Japan, which led to the founding of Japanese WCTU in 1886. After tour stops in Hawaii, New Zealand, and Australia, Leavitt arrived in Yokohama in June 1886.[18] The WWCTU efforts in Japan complemented American desires to open Japan to American commerce. A belief in American superiority and a conviction that the United States had a "God-given" duty to share its ideas and institutions provided enough cover for economic motivations.

Leavitt traveled across Japan promoting temperance and attempting to gain local support. She never learned Japanese and always used a translator when giving her speeches. Leavitt's refusal to learn Japanese demonstrates the imperialistic attitude of the temperance movement and the reformers belief that they had the morally superior position. The WWCTU's global movement pushed for reforming the empire with an emphasis on Anglo-American culture being dominant, while saving other cultures from the evils of alcohol.

---

16. Tyrrell, *Woman's World Women's Empire*, 147.

17. Tyrrell, *Woman's World Women's Empire*, 13.

18. Elizabeth Dorn Lublin, *Reforming Japan: The Women's Christian Temperance Union in the Meiji Period* (Vancouver: University of British Columbia Press, 2010), 23.

But WWCTU efforts floundered. In Japan, Leavitt had to shift her message away from religious discourse to scientific and empirical arguments after her attempts to convert Japanese crowds to Protestant Christianity failed.[19] She quickly learned that she drew far more people if she stressed temperance as a strategy to improve the Japanese nation. Leavitt inspired Iwamoto Yoshiharu, the second son of a low-level samurai, who had converted to Christianity earlier in 1883. He promoted Leavitt's talks and encouraged large numbers of women to attend. These efforts led to the creation of the Tokyo WCTU on December 6, 1886.[20]

Iwamoto converted to Christianity in 1883 due to his friendship and association with Kimura Kumaji, an American trained minister, and his wife Kimura Toko. The comparatively high status and educational opportunities for women in the United States impressed the Kimuras. After being introduced to Leavitt by Iwamoto, Kimura Toko became active in the temperance movement. She established, with thirteen other Japanese women—several of whom were the wives of Japanese ministers—the Tokyo WCTU.[21] The new chapter of the WWCTU started with a hundred members and promoted not only temperance, but overall moral reform of Japanese society.

The founding of the Tokyo WCTU occurred during the Meiji Restoration, which transformed Japanese politics, industry, and society. The Meiji Restoration restored authority to the Empire of Japan in 1868. Japan quickly modernized and industrialized to compete with the Western powers. In this transformative period, temperance reformers decided to improve the status of women and morally reform Japan based on Christian values. The Japanese founders, while Protestant, decided to drop Christian from the name and stress more universal notions of personal and societal morality. They renamed the organization the Women's Moral Reform Society (WMRS). To them, temperance consisted of only a small part of the overall goals of the new society. Despite the change in name, members of the WMRS carried on the work of the Anglo-American Protestant women who had recruited them.

By the late nineteenth century Anglo-American temperance leaders, many of whom were women, began to advocate for a total prohibition of alcohol. But given that many of their fellow male citizens regularly consumed alcohol and therefore could not be counted on as allies, women temperance leaders began to agitate for the right to vote. They argued that a political voice increased their ability to protect women and children and to extend the civilizing mission into formal political spaces. This idea became part of the international movement as well, with groups like the WWCTU pushing for more protection of women as

19. Lublin, *Reforming Japan*, 25.

20. Lublin, *Reforming Japan*, 33.

21. Lublin, *Reforming Japan*, 30.

part of reforming the empire. Many reformers believed that one of the first acts of newly enfranchised women would be voting to ban alcohol. Brewers and distillers realized this, and they campaigned heavily against women's suffrage. The shift of temperance groups into the area of politics and medicine proved to be effective, as the movement became the most well-organized lobby group of the time.

While temperance became a global movement, prohibition did not. Those countries that did ban alcohol did so with only limited success. So why examine prohibition? First, the goal of the temperance movement was the prohibition of alcohol to accomplish the civilizing mission. As we discovered with the temperance movement, much of the impetus in Europe and North America came from moralistic convictions of Evangelical Protestants. Newly empowered suffragettes strongly supported policies that curbed alcohol consumption at home and abroad. But a relatively lukewarm enthusiasm for Anglo-American Protestant values among colonized populations ultimately checked the possibilities for a global ban on alcohol. Colonial subjects simply did not prioritize alcohol as a primary cause of their misery. Rather, it was the colonial powers themselves that they began to identify, in concrete and emotionally powerful terms, as the culprits.

Second, reformers did not achieve prohibition in large part because of intense pressure from the economic interests that profited from the continued production, circulation, and consumption of alcohol. Since global trade routes for the circulation of alcohol and other drugs were fully established, prohibition failed to extend beyond a handful of places. Still, a few examples of the partial success of prohibition are instructive.

The WCTU heavily pushed for prohibition in Canada and succeeded in a limited way in 1878, with the passage the Canada Temperance Act. The Act provided the option for local prohibition. Any county or city in Canada could put prohibition of alcohol on the ballot if 25 percent of the electors signed a petition.[22] Once on the ballot, the measure needed a simple majority to institute prohibition in that locality. The first prohibition measure on Prince Edward Island did not pass until 1907, while other regions did not pass prohibition until 1916. Why did it take so long? In 1923 the sociologist Cyril Boyce highlighted the development and failure of prohibition in Canada, which gives us insight into the process at the time.[23] The local option measure allowed each area to define what type of alcohol to ban. Citizens in some areas outlawed the sale of beer and wine, but not hard liquors, while others did the reverse. The manufacturing of alcohol also continued in most areas for export. The Canadian economy depended on the manufacture and sale of alcohol for the global market, so while

22. Cyril D. Boyce, "Prohibition in Canada," *Annals of the American Academy of Political and Social Science* 109 (1923): 225.

23. Boyce, "Prohibition in Canada," 225.

temperance gained ground locally, the movement could not stop production because of its economic importance.

National prohibition finally passed in 1918 because of World War I, as many Canadian officials argued that prohibition would benefit the war effort since it prevented waste and inefficiency by limiting drunkenness. Some temperance reformers considered the barroom a location where "foreigners" congregated and "plotted" against the British Empire and the war effort.[24] Former opponents of prohibition fell silent so to avoid charges being unpatriotic. Manufacturing and export of alcohol continued and after World War I ended, most provinces repealed prohibition in the 1920s.

Despite concerted efforts to outlaw alcohol in the United States, which was in many ways in the vanguard of the movement, Iceland became the first to pass national prohibition in 1909. Iceland's law did not take effect until 1915, to allow for liquor distributors time to sell their remaining stocks, and full prohibition lasted until 1922.[25] Iceland exemplifies the marginal nature of prohibition and its failure to become a global movement, as only a few areas adopted the Anglo-American moral message. This moral message influenced public opinion in Iceland, as reformers argued that alcohol sales needed to be stopped to morally improve Icelandic society, but lost power when subjected to the pressures of international trade. Iceland did not have an alcohol manufacturing industry, instead relying on imports from other countries; Iceland's government modified the law because of economic pressure from Spanish authorities, who demanded that Iceland resume importation of Spanish wine in return for continued Spanish purchase of Icelandic fish.[26] We can see that frequently the economic pressures overwhelmed moral reform. This change opened the door to a debate on prohibition, with the government allowing hard liquor to be imported and sold in 1935. The government would continue to ban beer, as reformers argued that it could be manufactured in Iceland and being the cheapest alcohol would be harmful to workers and youth of Iceland. The importation of beer consisted of only a small part of the economy and did not threaten any international markets so the ban on beer continued until 1989.

The WCTU and the temperance movement in the United States influenced and inspired temperance reformers in Norway. The efforts of a few Norwegian reformers drew the attention of the WWCTU, and Frances Willard traveled to Norway in 1896 to promote their movement.[27] The WWCTU then formed a

---

24. Okrent, *Last Call*, 146.

25. Helgi Gunnlaugsson and John F. Galliher, "Prohibition of Beer in Iceland: An International Test of Symbolic Politics," *Law & Society Review* 20, no. 3 (1986): 339.

26. Gunnlaugsson and Galliher, "Prohibition of Beer in Iceland," 339.

27. Tyrell, *Women's World Women's Empire*, 263.

Norwegian chapter and supporters started to push for prohibition, adopting the Protestant Christian moral message of Anglo-American reformers. A major factor in the support of the WWCTU in Norway stemmed from the active participation of women. At the end of the nineteenth century, Norwegian women began to demand expanded political participation.[28] Some individuals looked at the women of the WCTU as role models of female activism. However, the WWCTU's Norwegian chapter gained little traction until the outbreak of World War I.

Norwegian anti-alcohol activists saw their chance with the outbreak of World War I, as the government supported the idea of prohibition because of the fear of wartime shortages of grain, potatoes, sugar, and salt (staples in the manufacture of alcohol).[29] The idea of limiting drunkenness and thereby reducing violence and petty crimes also appealed to segments of society. Norway, inspired by Anglo-American temperance arguments, had initial government support because of the war but also had the support of varied groups, including rural evangelical groups and radical workers groups from the industrial areas, due to the growth of socialism. While these groups approached the issue from different motives, they all agreed that prohibiting alcohol would be beneficial. National prohibition took effect in 1917, but governmental support only lasted until the end of the war in 1918. After World War I ended, Norway's economy experienced growing pressure from wine-producing countries, led by France. Like Spanish pressure upon Iceland, French authorities coerced Norway to end prohibition of wine or France would stop all imports of Norwegian fish.[30] This threat to a major Norwegian export forced the government to end prohibition on wine in 1921. This opened the door for beer and liquor manufacturers across Europe to persuade the governments as well, and many countries ended prohibition in 1927. Economic pressure once again overwhelmed moral crusades.

The temperance movement had little impact in the Russian Empire; however, they did introduce limited prohibition in 1914 by banning the sale of hard liquor (restaurants were excluded). The government decided on this restriction at the beginning of World War I under the premise that it would limit drunkenness of military personnel.[31] Controlling soldiers' behavior and making the military more efficient motivated prohibition in Russia rather than the moral aspects. In 1917 the Bolsheviks (Russian Marxists)[32] seized control of the government in Russia

28. Tyrell, *Women's World Women's Empire*, 253.

29. Per Ole Johansen, "The Norwegian Alcohol Prohibition; A Failure," *Journal of Scandinavian Studies in Criminology and Crime Prevention* 14, no. Supplement I (2013): 47.

30. Johansen, "Norwegian Alcohol Prohibition," 48.

31. Neil Weissman, "Prohibition and Alcohol Control in the USSR: The 1920s Campaign against Illegal Spirits," *Soviet Studies* 38, no. 3 (1986): 350.

32. The Bolsheviks followed the ideas of Karl Marx and led a Marxist Revolution in Russia, later renaming themselves communist.

in the October Revolution. Shortly after this, in November and December, several liquor riots broke out in Petrograd, led mainly by soldiers. The new government quickly reinforced the ban on hard liquor and destroyed supplies of vodka.[33] During the 1920s the government (now known as the Union of Soviet Socialist Republics or Soviet Union) sporadically enforced the ban, and it completely ended in 1925. Ultimately, financial concerns and the failure to end the illegal production and importation of vodka forced the Soviets to eliminate prohibition. The Anglo-American moral Protestant message gained little traction in Russia.

In 1919 the US Congress passed the Volstead Act, which empowered the federal government and states to carry out the provisions of the eighteenth amendment, which regulated the "manufacture, sale, or transportation of intoxicating liquors within the United States" and prohibited consumption of certain intoxicating beverages. Both the amendment and the act were, in the eyes of many moral reformers, the grandest achievement of decades of work. National prohibition was now a reality. However, most Americans did not actually support the new law. The WCTU and other reformers proved to be more powerful lobbying organizations than persuaders of popular opinion. Demand for alcohol beverages continued, but now it was illegal in most cases. So while manufacturing and selling alcohol became illegal in the United States, the global market still provided the product, and illegal production emerged inside US borders. Prohibition in the United States provides an example of not only the limitations of the global movement, but of the power of the global markets for alcohol that had been established. Since overall demand did not decrease and trade routes were firmly established, an illegal market supplied liquor to meet the demand.

What were the impacts of prohibition in the United States? Scholars still debate the long-term effects of alcohol prohibition. Some argue that drinking and drinking-related health problems declined. Others argue that alcohol consumption increased as an illegal trade developed. Did prohibition decrease alcohol consumption? Was prohibition in the United States successful overall? Mark H. Moore, professor at the Kennedy School of Government, contends that alcohol consumption declined dramatically during Prohibition. He argues that cirrhosis death rates, arrests for public drunkenness, and alcohol consumption all declined.[34] Jack S. Blocker Jr., a historian at Huron College, agrees with this assessment, insisting that death rates from cirrhosis and alcoholism, hospital admissions, and arrests for drunkenness all declined steeply during the early years of Prohibition.[35] On the other hand, Michael Lerner, a professor at Harvard

---

33. Weissman, "Prohibition and Alcohol Control in the USSR," 350.

34. Mark H. Moore, *Alcohol and Public Policy: Beyond the Shadow of Prohibition* (Washington, DC: National Academies Press, 1981), 14.

35. Jack S. Blocker, "Did Prohibition Really Work? Alcohol Prohibition as a Public Health Innovation," *American Journal of Public Health* 96, no. 2 (2006): 235.

University, disagrees and states that while a decline in medical and social problems occurred, overall Prohibition failed.[36] Lerner demonstrates that the ultimate goals of Prohibition never occurred, as reformers claimed commerce in other products would increase but the expected boom did not happen. The economic losses of alcohol production and taxes was also substantial. Lerner claims that the increase in law enforcement costs and the increase in criminal activity and organized crime became unintended consequences. While drinking and health problems declined, most of these gains occurred in the early years of the law's enforcement. The creation of the illegal trade in alcohol became the main result of Prohibition. After the illegal market became established, many of the early gains disappeared.

Opium Eaters and Cocaine Cowboys: Ending the Menace

As was the case with attempts to ban alcohol, Anglo-American efforts at moral reform drove the anti-opium movement as well. As we explored in chapters 2 and 3, opium had developed into a major global commodity, with imperialism and the opium trade fully intertwined. Protestant moral reform provided the foundation for the anti-opium movement. In Great Britain the Pharmaceutical Society examined moral reform, stating that the poor of England overused opium and morphine due to a lack of moral resolve (See Figure 4.2).[37] The society pushed for more control, resulting in the Poisons and Pharmacy Act of 1868, which regulated the sale of opium and morphine. In the 1890s this act aimed to regulate the sale of patent medicines containing opium and cocaine. The United States moved toward more control as well.

Attempts to regulate and prohibit opium were not just national projects, but imperial as well. In the British Empire, the Society for the Suppression of the Opium Trade (SSOT) promoted the anti-opium movement with the goal of reforming and civilizing colonial populations in Asia. The SSOT, formed in London in November 1874, campaigned against the opium trade in India and China, but stopped short of any sustained critique of British imperialism in Asia more broadly. These moral reformers believed in the superiority of British culture and couched that superiority in efforts to protect allegedly weaker colonial populations from the potential excesses of imperialism, including opiates.[38] In turn, the SSOT argued, the elimination of opium would make the British Empire

---

36. Michael Lerner, *Dry Manhattan: Prohibition in New York City* (Cambridge, MA: Harvard University Press, 2008).

37. Virginia Berridge, *Demons: Our Changing Attitudes to Alcohol, Tobacco, and Drugs* (New York: Oxford University Press, 2013), 57.

38. J. B. Brown, "Politics of the Poppy: The Society for the Suppression of the Opium Trade, 1874–1916," *Journal of Contemporary History* 8, no. 3 (1973): 98.

FIGURE 4.2 Opium smokers in the East End of London. Reformers were concerned with the social impact of the drug.
Source: Opium smokers in the East End of London, 1874. From the Illustrated London News, 1 August 1874/Wikipedia.

more efficient and productive. The society understood that economic expansion and trade drove the empire, and they believed that opium was the source of a stagnation of "legitimate" exports to China. Reformers argued that the opium trade depleted foreign currency reserves in China, and English cotton manufacturers would increase their exports to China fivefold by abolishing the drug trade. As we can see, the society argued that other areas of commerce would improve if drugs decreased their market share. Reformers also blamed opium for the limited progress in spreading Christianity in China.[39] The Anglo-American moral reform of the empire depended on the spread of Christianity. Businessmen involved in the opium trade felt threatened by the anti-opium movement; however, they had the support of the press and government policy.[40] As we discussed in earlier chapters, the opium trade had a huge global economic impact.

By the 1880s, opium became one of the most valuable commodities moving in international trade. In an average year opium exported from Calcutta and Bombay averaged over 90,000 chests (5,400 metric tons), with between 13 and

39. Brown, "Politics of the Poppy," 102.

40. Martin Booth, *Opium: A History* (New York: St. Martin's Press, 1998), 153.

14 million opium consumers in China and Southeast Asia.[41] Opium exports equaled 16 percent of the official revenues of British India, leading pro-opium advocates to argue that opium had a limited negative impact and that it represented an important part of India's economy. As opium traffic increased, reformers increased their efforts to limit the trade, slowly gaining support in England.

Opium trade supporters feared that the Christian missionaries of the SSOT would convince the government to end the trade. In order to lessen the impact of the reform movement, the pro-opium advocates used the case of Reverend F. Galpin of the English Methodist Free Church in Ningpo, China, to argue that not all Christian missionaries supported an end to the trade.[42] Galpin argued that the government and people of China did not want to end the opium trade, and that stopping the importation of opium from British India would have little effect in China. His position centered on the idea that if China wanted an end to opium, the sovereign government there would have already done so. But as we learned in chapter 3, this is not supported by the evidence. On more than one occasion Chinese authorities tried to stop the trade in opium but repeatedly failed due to Great Britain's interference. The anti-opium reformers successfully countered this position, as Galpin represented the only missionary to support opium.[43]

The 1890s saw the creation of a coalition forged between globally oriented pressure groups. While the SSOT was a driving force, local groups arose that started to work together on a global scale. One of these groups, Sharada Saran, worked toward protecting Hindu women and girls in India.[44] A major part of this help consisted of attempting to end the impact of opium. Soonderbai H. Powar became the leader of this group and she rose to prominence in the anti-opium campaign in India, organizing a global coalition with support from English Quakers and English anti-opium businessmen as well as her local followers.[45] Sharada Saran worked with the SSOT to try and end opium production in India.

The public pressure generated by the SSOT forced the British Parliament to create the Royal Commission on Opium in 1893. In 1893, the Royal Commission faced a well-organized anti-opium opposition with connections in India, China, and Britain.[46] The Royal Commission examined the opium trade from India to China

---

41. John F. Richards, "Opium and the British Indian Empire: The Royal Commission of 1895," *Modern Asian Studies* 36, no. 2 (2002): 377.

42. Kathleen Lodwick, *Crusaders Against Opium: Protestant Missionaries in China, 1874–1917* (Lexington: University of Kentucky Press, 1996), 77.

43. Lodwick, *Crusaders Against Opium*, 79.

44. Steffen Rimner, *Opium's Long Shadow: From Asian Revolt to Global Drug Control* (Cambridge, MA: Harvard University Press, 2018), 84.

45. Rimner, *Opium's Long Shadow*, 87–88.

46. Rimner, *Opium's Long Shadow*, 131–32.

and its impact on the population of India. However, the Commission's report, published in 1895, dealt a blow to the efforts of anti-opium reformers, stating:

> As the result of a searching inquiry, and upon a deliberate review of the copious evidence submitted to us, we feel bound to express our conviction that the movement in England in favor of active interference on the part of the Imperial Parliament for the suppression of the opium habit in India, has proceeded from an exaggerated impression as to the nature and extent of the evil to be controlled. The gloomy descriptions presented to British audiences of extensive moral and physical degradation by opium have not been accepted by the witnesses representing the people of India, nor by those most responsible for the government of the country.[47]

What does this quote tell us? India suffered from opium, but the commission downplayed the problem. Why? One major reason could be that the opium trade, still important to British commerce, outweighed the anti-opium reform movement. The commission also considered the SSOT a small provincial group, without understanding its global organization. Another reason is that the Commission interviewed mostly Europeans and producers, not workers or Indians. The Royal Commission angered reformers, since they did not travel to China to examine the impact of opium production and use there. The Commission did not examine the growing opium production in China, which quickly became central to the global opium trade. As a result, prohibition efforts would not gain ground for another ten years. The meaning and impact of the Royal Commission on opium has divided historians. Historians generally agree that the commission was a landmark event, but divided into two main positions on the interpretation of that event. One position evaluates its political, social, and ideological impact, while the second position attempts to understand the driving forces behind its decisions.[48] Both positions attempt to shed light on the complexities of the opium trade.

While Anglo-American reform attempted to end the opium trade in China, the Japanese government decided to end what they saw as the Chinese opium threat. By the 1860s farmers in Japan grew poppies, but almost all production consisted of medicinal use only.[49] The Japanese government watched the Opium

---

47. Great Britain, Sessional Papers of the House of Commons, XLII, Final Report of the Royal Commission on Opium, 1894, Cornell University, https://archive.org/details/cu31924073053864/page/n93, 97.

48. Rimner, *Opium's Long Shadow*, 148.

49. Bob Tadashi Wakabayashi, "From Peril to Profit: Opium in Late Edo to Meiji Eyes," in *Opium Regimes: China, Britain and Japan 1839–1952,* ed. Timothy Brook and Bob Tadashi Wakabayashi (Berkeley: University of California Press, 2000), 66.

Wars in China with growing concern. Government officials worried about future imperial pressure from Western powers and saw opium as a forerunner of this imperialism. The number of Chinese immigrants living in Japan also grew, which raised largely unfounded fears about an impending opium epidemic. In 1868, the new Meiji government began to regulate opium production and distribution by restricting it solely to medicinal use. Anyone who sold opium or tried to encourage opium smoking was executed. The government regulated all medical supplies and by 1876 controlled imports. Foreign producers could only sell opium directly to the Meiji government. Japanese authorities took very early steps to control and regulate opium long before other nations accomplished the goal. In large part, they did so to prevent further incursion of European and American economic interests that could, if unregulated, threaten the reforms and projects that the Meiji government championed.

As we explained in chapter 2, manufacturers introduced cocaine to the global market in the late nineteenth century. Since cocaine entered the market later than opium, resistance to the drug did not grow until the early twentieth century. By this time, the global trade in medical and recreational cocaine stretched from Peru and other South American countries across Europe, Japan, India, Egypt, and the United States.[50] The growing trade and increased use sparked local drug scenes and panics. Medical and popular attitudes on cocaine started to change in the 1890s, with the zeal of American anti-cocaine reformers driving the change. In the United States pharmaceutical and chemical companies sold cocaine in a variety of coca products. Coca-Cola and other soft drink companies also popularized the use of coca leaves. However, US medical authorities did not have the enthusiasm for cocaine as a wonder drug that European medical authorities did. As cocaine use spread in the early twentieth century, due to overproduction and dropping prices, reformers started associating the drug with addiction, prostitution, and criminal activities. Race, especially in the US South, also played a critical role. Many reformers argued that cocaine affected African Americans differently than white consumers (including an increased propensity toward violence), thereby tying racial fears to the need to restrict the drug.[51] This is another example of the push by white Christian reformers to implement the civilizing mission at home. After 1900, stories spread of "black cocaine fiends" committing a variety of criminal offenses. Anti-cocaine reformers harnessed racism and racial stereotypes of the period to promote their campaign. Anti-cocaine state and local initiatives spread, and the stage was set for an Anglo-American drive to ban cocaine.

---

50. Paul Gootenberg, *Andean Cocaine: The Making of a Global Drug* (Chapel Hill: University of North Carolina Press, 2008), 122.

51. Gootenberg, *Andean Cocaine*, 193.

The Society for the Suppression of Opium had suffered a huge setback with the publication of the Royal Commission's report. But they persisted, and in 1906 they pushed forward a slate of two hundred Parliamentary candidates who supported an end to the opium trade.[52] While many of the candidates lost their elections, political opinion in Britain shifted in favor of prohibition. Authorities in Great Britain declared that if China wanted to restrict opium, they would be supportive. The Chinese government, which had wanted to stop opium use for decades, quickly issued an imperial decree to end all opium smoking and close opium dens. The Chinese government announced its intention to end the use of opium in China by 1917.

Reformers next focused on India, and British officials in India signed a ten-year agreement with China to phase out opium exports and production. The reason officials wanted to have a ten-year process was to limit the disruption to agriculture in India. Peasant farmers had become dependent on growing opium poppies, since they were easy to grow and provided a higher cash return. The ten-year reduction allowed for the British officials to introduce other cash crops into India. Fields dedicated to opium poppy production declined, and in 1909 India stopped all opium exports. Legal opium production ended in China in 1917, but this did not stop opium use. As was the case with alcohol in the United States and other countries that tried prohibition, illegal markets quickly appeared.

In Peru, the leading supplier of coca leaves and raw cocaine for the US market and German pharmaceutical companies, the European and Mestizo[53] population worried about the impact of cocaine on the indigenous population. The concept that the native people of Peru were inferior to those of European descent came from the Spanish colonial period. This idea is a part of the imperial mindset, like the Anglo-American moral superiority. Hermilio Valdizan, a leading Peruvian psychiatrist, became one of the first prominent twentieth-century critics to propose a national policy for eradicating the use of coca.[54] He argued that cocaine and coca, not alcohol, caused what he termed Indian "degeneration." Valdizan published his findings in 1910, stating that cocaine addicts represented the largest medical and social threat to Peru. He proposed that the Peruvian government prevent owners of coca plantations from paying native workers with coca leaves or using them as incentives. Although Valdizan failed to convince the government of the threat due to the economic importance of the cocaine industry, he did start an anti-cocaine movement in Peru.[55] Other Peruvian elites and medical

---

52. Booth, *Opium*, 157.

53. Mestizos are individuals of mixed European (mostly Spanish) and indigenous descent.

54. Joseph A. Gagliano, *Coca Prohibition in Peru: The Historical Debates* (Tucson: University of Arizona Press, 1994), 121.

55. Gagliano, *Cocaine Prohibition in Peru*, 122.

authorities joined Valdizan in denouncing cocaine. Pentecostal missionaries, led by the Seventh-Day Adventists from the United States, picked up on the local movement and promoted an end to the coca market to protect and reform the native population. These US missionaries represented a form of American cultural imperialism, as they pushed the idea that American values were superior to those of the local native peoples. The Peruvian anti-cocaine movement, which started locally, would become part of the larger Anglo-American moral reform of native populations.

The Anglo-American reformation of the empire continued in 1909 with the convening of the Shanghai Opium Smoking Conference, which marked a new era in opium policy.[56] The United States, a driving force behind the conference, convened the thirteen-nation conference in Shanghai, China, pushing for an international ban on the opium trade. These nations then formed the Shanghai Opium Commission, which American reformers argued should have the power to enforce regulations; however, participating governments only allowed it to make recommendations. The Commission had little power, but it did make several recommendations, and for the first time provided a detailed global overview of the world's drug trade. They reported total opium production at around 41,600 metric tons. China produced 85 percent of this total, India 12 percent, and Persia (modern-day Iran), accounted for 1.5 percent.[57] As we can see, the Shanghai meeting clearly demonstrated the extent of the global trade in opium. The largest exporter of opium at the time was India, followed by Hong Kong and Singapore, which did not produce opium but re-exported the drug. The Shanghai Opium Commission laid the groundwork for the next international conference in 1911 at The Hague, Netherlands.

The next conference not only looked at smoking opium but at medicinal opium, prepared opium products, morphine, and cocaine. The result led to the first international drug control treaty, the International Opium Convention, signed at The Hague on January 23, 1912, which stated: "The contracting Powers shall use their best endeavors to control, or to cause to be controlled, all persons manufacturing, importing, selling, distributing, and exporting morphine, cocaine, and their respective salts, as well as the buildings in which these persons carry such an industry or trade."[58] If we examine this excerpt, it acknowledges that opium and cocaine had global implications and needed to be controlled on an international level. While thirty-four nations participated in the International

56. Ashley Wright, *Opium and Empire in Southeast Asia: Regulating Consumption in British Burma* (New York: Palgrave McMillian, 2014), 95.

57. Lodwick, *Crusaders Against Opium*, 101.

58. League of Nations, *Treaty Series* Vol. 8 (1922), United Nations Treaty Series, https://treaties.un.org/Pages/LONOnline.aspx?clang=_en, 187.

Opium Convention, getting all these nations to agree to ratify the treaty remained a daunting task. Over the next thirty months, efforts by the US State Department, British Foreign Office, and the Dutch government produced only eight ratifications and twenty-four promises to adhere to the treaty.[59] When World War I broke out in August 1914, more pressing issues dominated the attention of many countries.

Since international global action slowly developed, due to the economic power of the producers of these drugs, a few countries decided to work within their own borders. The United States, China, the Netherlands, and Honduras all put the International Opium Convention into force. It is clear why China and the United States worked to ban opium from our previous discussions—but why the Netherlands and Honduras? The Netherlands supported the Convention under some US economic pressure, but the Dutch government's desire to control the opium and cocaine market within their borders and to create a state-run opium market was the main reason.[60] To the Dutch authorities, limiting opium meant controlling the market, not outright prohibition. Honduras also supported opium restriction under pressure from United States. American fruit companies dominated Honduran economics in the early twentieth century and the US government thereby forced them to support the convention, highlighting another example of American imperialism.

Drug use increased during World War I, leading to increased efforts for international controls. After the war ended, British and American delegates to the Paris Peace Conference required a clause for ratification of the International Opium Convention be included in all peace treaties, representing another example of Anglo-American efforts for controlling the drug trade.[61] China also insisted that Germany and Austria adhere to the Convention as a condition for peace. The League of Nations, founded on January 10, 1920, assumed responsibility for international drug control. The League of Nations became the first international organization whose principle mission was to maintain world peace. That the League was tasked to control the global drug trade is another representation of the globalization of law and politics in relation to society and commerce.

Pharmaceutical companies in Germany produced most of the morphine, heroin, and cocaine for the world market in the prewar years, which ended with the outbreak of war. As a result, manufacturers in England, France, and Japan increased their own pharmaceutical facilities while expanding cocaine

---

59. William B. McAllister, *Drug Diplomacy in the Twentieth Century: An International History* (London: Routledge, 2000), 35.

60. Marcel De Kort and Dirk J. Korf, "The Development of Drug Trade and Drug Control in the Netherlands: A Historical Perspective," *Crime, Law and Social Change* 17 (1992): 130.

61. McAllister, *Drug Diplomacy*, 36.

manufacturing. Each government therefore desired to control and regulate medical opium and cocaine while limiting importation, production, and recreational use of these drugs. By 1920, the cultural preferences and power of the Western industrialized nations determined which drugs escaped limitation and which suffered restrictions.[62] However, due to the abundant supplies of opiates and cocaine and the demand created by industrialization and commercialization, a thriving illegal global market for these drugs expanded.

The Rise of Global Illegal Markets

The illegal market in alcohol that developed during Prohibition in the United States provides an instructive example of the continuation of one type of global commerce. Since US alcohol prohibition banned the sale, manufacture, and import of alcoholic beverages but not the consumption of them, the demand for alcohol continued. As legal supplies diminished, people turned to medical and religious exceptions in the law. Certain individuals realized the economic opportunity and started to provide alcohol using these exceptions. As the US government tightened these restrictions, many Americans turned to producing their own alcohol. This "bootlegging" continued throughout Prohibition; however, as demand grew, the illegal suppliers needed more product than bootlegging alone could provide. Suppliers turned to "rum running" (smuggling), importing large amounts of alcohol from international producers. Large-scale transportation networks created before US Prohibition continued to provide alcohol to US markets. The primary evolution here was that of new organizations in the United States interacting with the international suppliers. Before Prohibition, large import/export companies handled the supply of liquor. After Prohibition, organized crime syndicates fulfilled that role.

Alcohol production continued in the Caribbean Islands, with the islands becoming a way station for liquor produced in European countries. For example, smugglers developed regular supply lines from Bimini, Bahamas into South Florida. Bill McCoy, one of the more famous of these rum-runners, became known for the quality and amount of his smuggled liquor. As the Coast Guard cracked down on the shipments, the smugglers created "rum rows" along the coasts of the United States. Rum rows consisted of large boats from the Caribbean and Europe just outside the three-mile limit of US jurisdiction. The suppliers then used smaller boats and local fishermen to run the liquor into the country. The small, quick boats easily outran Coast Guard ships and could dock in any small river or eddy and transfer their cargo to waiting trucks. On April 21, 1924, the United States Congress extended US waters to a twelve-mile limit,

---

62. McAllister, *Drug Diplomacy*, 38.

to make it harder for the smaller craft to make the trip.[63] Other rum-runners often made the trip through Canada via the Great Lakes and the Saint Lawrence Seaway, and down the east coast and across the Detroit River. The French islands of Saint-Pierre and Miquelon, located south of Newfoundland, became an important base for smuggling (See Map 4.1). As the illegal trade in alcohol grew and became more complex, organizations needed more employees and money. Organized crime syndicates dominated the trade and kept the supply of alcohol flowing. It became increasingly obvious to US citizens and many reformers that the supply of liquor was unabated and with the rise of organized crime, support for Prohibition ended. The United States repealed Prohibition on December 5, 1933, with the twenty-first Amendment ending the national attempt stop alcohol consumption.

Meanwhile, the League of Nations had taken charge of supervising global opium and cocaine restrictions incurred with the Convention treaties. The League created the Advisory Committee on Traffic in Opium and Other Dangerous Drugs (OAC) in 1920, but those government officials favoring strict drug control doubted whether the League possessed the political will to enact strict drug control measures.[64] The United States government made it clear that they held both producing and manufacturing states responsible for escalating international drug problems and also made multilateral action against drugs difficult to achieve, because they held foreigners responsible, if not accountable, for any problems that impaired US anti-drug efforts. In the early 1920s manufacturers in the United States, Japan, and Europe dominated production of these drugs. The US Congress tried to control the export of manufactured drugs with the Narcotic Drugs Import and Export Act of 1922, which required exporters to possess proper certificates from the destination country before importing (See Figure 4.3). Congress amended the act in 1924 to prohibit opium importation for the manufacture of heroin, which they saw as the major problem. The United States meant this to serve as a model for other countries, but heroin manufactured outside the United States continued to enter the illegal international market.

Manufacturing states did not want to cede control of importing drugs to the United States, as it would mean a loss of market share. So the US government attempted to stop the drug supply by focusing on the drug-producing nations. This proved to be difficult because the collapse of the Chinese Empire after 1915 led to a decade of internal strife dominated by regional warlords, making efforts to halt poppy growing impossible. Opium played a vital role in China's economy during the warlord era. As for cocaine, many urban users in the United States switched to heroin as a cheaper drug of choice after scarcity and strict

---

63. Everett Allen, *The Black Ships: Rumrunners of Prohibition* (Boston: Little, Brown, 2015), 74.

64. Brook and Wakabayashi, *Opium Regimes*, 43.

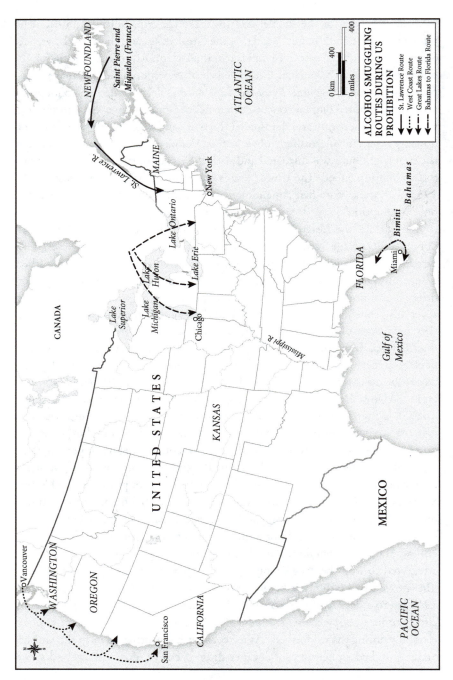

MAP 4.1 Alcohol Smuggling Routes During US Prohibition

THE POOR CHILD'S NURSE.

FIGURE 4.3 Anti-opium reformers used images such as this to illustrate the effect of the drug on children. Poor child's nurse, child with opium, Punch, 1849.
Source: Wellcome Collection. Attribution 4.0 International (CC BY 4.0)

enforcement of state laws drove up black-market prices for cocaine. US officials then encouraged Andean nations to move toward gradual compliance with international agreements regarding coca production, supporting the work being done by Andean prohibitionists.[65] Stopping production in Peru and Bolivia had limited success, since coca represented a part of the national culture and many farmers grew the crop. The attempts to control drugs had only limited success, as once the legal market for recreational use ended, an illegal international trade replaced it. Full drug prohibition was never attempted, as medical and other select trade in opiates and cocaine continued. We can see from this that while not the only participant, the United States had become a leader in global drug regulation and control, stemming from the Anglo-American attempts to reform empire. This movement of the United States to a major player on the world stage continued and increased with World War II. The United States then became the primary proponent for opiate and cocaine restriction by developing the global war on drugs, which further exemplifies the continued development of America as an empire.

---

65. Gagliano, *Coca Prohibition in Peru*, 135.

FURTHER READING

Fallaw, Ben. "Dry Law, Wet Politics: Drinking and Prohibition in Post-Revolutionary Yucatan, 1915–1935." *Latin American Research Review* 37, no. 2 (2002): 37–64.

Gootenberg, Paul. *Andean Cocaine: The Making of a Global Drug.* Chapel Hill: University of North Carolina Press, 2008.

Lublin, Elizabeth Dorn. *Reforming Japan: The Women's Christian Temperance Union in the Meiji Period.* Vancouver: University of British Columbia Press, 2010.

McCoy, Alfred. "From Free Trade to Prohibition: A Critical History of the Modern Asian Opium Trade." *Fordham Urban Law Journal* 28, no. 1 (2000): 307–49.

Wright, Ashley. *Opium and Empire in Southeast Asia: Regulating Consumption in British Burma.* New York: Palgrave McMillian, 2014.

5

POSTWAR GLOBALIZATION

COLD WAR EMPIRES AND DRUG WARS

In 1945, after World War II, France continued to control Vietnam, Laos, and Cambodia (French Indochina). Vietnamese nationalists, seeking independence and led by Ho Chi Minh, rebelled against the French forces. In previous chapters we explored the actions of the Western imperial powers. But after World War II, resistance to colonialism grew behind similar nationalist movements that developed in colonies around the world. Ho Chi Minh's forces (the Viet Minh) wanted the French out of Vietnam. However, their communist ideology complicated the issue. The key aspect of this struggle, as it pertains to this book, consisted of the involvement of French officials and organized crime syndicates in the illegal opium trade across Southeast Asia. Vietnamese communists considered this trade the ultimate example of French colonial exploitation. They used the problems surrounding opium use and addiction in the region as a propaganda tool. Interestingly, they used a description of an opium den written by the French writer Andrée Viollis (a reporter for the newspaper *Le Petit Parisien*) to demonstrate not only opium's destructive impact on the local population, but to highlight the hypocrisy of the French officials.[1]

Just past the entrance, a horrible odor of corruption strikes your throat. The corridor turns, turns again, and opens on several small dark rooms, which become veritable labyrinths lighted by lamps which give off a troubled yellow light. The walls, caked with dirt, are indented with long niches. In each niche a man is spread out like a stone. Nobody moves when we pass. Not even a glance. They are glued to a small pipe whose watery gurgle alone breaks the silence. The others are terribly immobile, with slow gestures, legs strung out, arms in the air, as if they had been struck dead . . . The faces are characterized by overly white teeth; the pupils with a black glaze, enlarged, fixed

---

1. Alfred McCoy, *The Politics of Heroin in Southeast Asia* (New York: Harper & Row, 1972), 75.

on god knows what; the eyelids do not move; and on the pasty cheeks, this vague, mysterious smile of the dead. It was an awful sight to see walking among there cadavers.[2]

If we examine this quote, the impact of opium on drug users in Vietnam seems clear. Why would Vietnamese communists use this account for propaganda? Opium use had a heavy impact on the people of the region and to gain support for their movement, Vietnamese communists argued that root of the problem lay in the French government's imperialism and global capitalism. In previous chapters we examined the role of imperialism and industrial capitalism in the globalization of the drug trade up to the early twentieth century. As we saw, these processes of globalization had a direct impact on people around the world. By the mid-century, communist rebels used this detrimental impact to generate support and demonstrate the damage of French rule. Many of Viollis's writings criticized French colonialism, so the Vietnamese communists used his writings to show the hypocrisy of French authorities. Vietnamese communists argued that French officials were fully aware of the problem but chose to ignore the damage due to their capitalist greed. Viollis's book highlighted that at least some French citizens were aware the problem. Nevertheless, French officials still participated in the drug trade.

In this chapter we will examine the role of the illegal drug trade during the Cold War and its relationship to post–World War II globalization that intertwined with the imperial actions of the United States and the Soviet Union. This chapter focuses on the expansion of the opium trade into Vietnam and Southeast Asia, and the development of a cocaine trade in Peru and Colombia. We will briefly review the role of free trade in the creation of the drug wars in Mexico as well. Decolonization after World War II and the struggle between capitalists and communists played a major role, as did the US government's creation of a "war on drugs" as an extension of American economic and cultural imperialism. The international dimensions of the war on drugs became a campaign, waged by the US government, of drug prohibition, military aid, and law enforcement intervention to reduce the trade in illegal drugs in the United States and internationally. The initiative included policies aimed at discouraging the production, distribution, and consumption of psychoactive drugs (including heroin and cocaine) declared illegal by the United Nations. Ironically, some US officials and agencies used drugs as a weapon against communism, while other American officials fought against the trade. We also need to remember the role of producers and sellers of these drugs.

To understand the international trade in drugs after World War II, it is necessary to first understand the actions of the Soviet Union and the United States in

---

2. Andrée Viollis, *Indochine S.O.S* (Paris: Gallimard, 1935), 17.

relation to the Cold War—a confrontation between the Soviet Union and its allies and the United States and its allies.[3] The Cold War leaders represented the conflict as an economic and ideological struggle, but was it a political struggle between two new powerful twentieth-century empires as well? As we will see, the United States and the Soviet Union both had cultures of imperialism. The struggle between these two superpowers manifested itself in rhetorical aggression. Political leaders in both nations attempted to manipulate this rhetoric to promote conformity within their own populations.[4] The ideologies of these two nation-states, whether anti-capitalist or anti-communist, was used to justify their interference around the world.

After World War II the United States became a major world power, replacing Great Britain as the leader of Western-style capitalism, promoting the idea of democracy, and becoming a driving force in global economic integration. The Union of Soviet Socialist Republics (USSR, also called the Soviet Union) also became a world power and the leader of communist ideology, spreading communism and their influence worldwide. The Soviet Union, with the second largest economy in the world, led opposition to Western capitalism and imperialism. The struggle between these two world powers and their allies formed the foundation of the Cold War.

The Cold War spread to Asia as well. After World War II, fighting between Mao Tse-tung and his communist forces and Chiang Kai-shek and his nationalist government (a continuation of the pre–World War II Chinese Civil War) increased tension in China. The US government supported Chiang's government against the communists. After the victory of Mao's forces in 1949 and the creation of the People's Republic of China, the US government worried that all of Asia would fall to communism. This fear increased when the Soviet-supported communist government of North Korea invaded US-occupied South Korea in 1950, setting off the Korean War, which lasted until 1953.

The governments of the Soviet Union and the United States competed for influence in Asian, Latin American, and African states that were moving toward independence from colonial powers after World War II. Across the world, nationalist movements pushed for the dismantlement of the Western empires of the early twentieth century. Nationalists, who advocated for the political independence of a nation or group of people, supported these decolonization efforts, which combined with European governments' economic collapse after World War II, led to the independence of the former colonies starting in the late 1940s. In order to spread their control, the US and Soviet governments attempted to

---

3. Heather Streets-Salter and Trevor Getz, *Empires and Colonies in the Modern World: A Global Perspective* (New York: Oxford University Press, 2016), 474.

4. Streets-Salter and Getz, *Empires and Colonies*, 482.

influence these newly independent countries. Many of these countries, known as Third World countries, attempted to stay neutral in the Cold War between the United States and other developed capitalist nations and the Soviet Union and other industrialized communist nations.[5]

Why did some nations and groups become allies of the Soviet Union and others with the United States? Part of the reason is linked to the imperialism of the early twentieth century. As European empires started to break apart after World War II, nationalists in these colonies pushed for independence. Many nations around the world had suffered heavy damages from the war. As Allied powers liberated countries from Germany or Japan and decolonization spread, people around the world looked for systems or ideologies that supported their concepts of independence. In some cases, Soviet communism's anti-capitalism appealed to nationalists as they moved out from under imperial capitalism, seeking self-determination. Others received economic aid from the United States and decided that capitalism was the path to economic power, thereby linking themselves to global capitalism.

So how did the politics of the Cold War relate to the globalization of illegal drugs? Illegal drugs became one of many tools in the politics and economy of empire as the new imperial powers fought proxy wars in drug-producing areas. In the early 1950s, the United States became a major market for heroin and cocaine. Why? Opiates and cocaine had been promoted by manufacturers as cure-alls. These addictive substances were then banned, but the demand still continued. After World War II the United States experienced many changes and while the economy boomed, the gains were not evenly distributed. The world under capitalism had also seen a cultural evolution in the spread in seeking pleasure and escape.[6] This combination of capitalism and the pleasurable escape from problems led to a growing demand for drugs. Many American officials believed that communists were using these illegal drugs to undermine American values and weaken the United States, and thus that Americans needed to protect themselves from such degenerate, outside influences. US government officials argued that foreigners drove the drug trade and encouraged drug use. US politicians stressed that the United States needed to protect not only its own citizens but the people of the world from communism, as well as heroin and cocaine. Drugs—both legal and illegal—became part of the arsenal that the US government used to wage war and spread American economic and cultural power to the world.[7] Ironically, some US officials and government agencies saw illegal drugs as a useful commodity to

5. See Carole Fink, *Cold War: An International History* (New York: Routledge, 2017).

6. David Courtwright, *The Age of Addiction: How Bad Habits Became Big Business* (Cambridge, MA: Harvard University Press, 2019), 6.

7. Suzanna Reiss, *We Sell Drugs: The Alchemy of US Empire* (Berkeley: University of California Press, 2014), 1.

fight the spread of communism. These individuals saw communism as the greatest threat and used the heroin and cocaine trade as just another tool to fight it. As we will see, some members of US agencies actively supported ant-communist groups that participated in the international trade in illegal drugs.

Drugs in World War II

Before we examine the Cold War drug trade, we need to briefly look at the illegal drug market in opium and cocaine during World War II. Before the start of the war, a major trade route for illegal heroin ran from Iran, India, and Turkey into France. Labs run by a Corsican-organized crime syndicate led by Paul Carbone and Francois Spirito supplied this heroin to Europe and the United States.[8] This heroin network became known as the French Connection. Farmers in Turkey, Iran, and India produced opium for sale to legal drug companies, but many sold their excess on the illegal market. Criminal syndicates refined the opium into heroin in Corsican laboratories in Marseille, France, which served as a perfect shipping point because of the frequent arrival of ships from opium-producing countries, bringing smuggled excess opium in with the legal shipments. The French underground then shipped heroin from Marseille to various locations, with New York City being a primary destination. The outbreak of World War II threatened to disrupt trade routes from Peru and Bolivia (bringing coca), and India and Turkey (supplying opium). As a result, international trade routes changed and shifted, allowing room for more trade routes for illegal drugs.

After the start of World War II, Corsican smugglers worried that opium trade routes from Iran and Turkey might be disrupted. They started looking at other areas to increase production. Afraid of losing their opium monopoly, the syndicate encouraged Hmong (an ethnic group living in Southeast Asia) farmers in French Indochina to expand opium production in that region. But Japanese military occupation of French Indochina in 1940 disrupted this production. With the end of World War II, French officials working with French and Corsican smugglers started illegally shipping opium from Indochina to Marseille. After the war the labs in Marseille also received opium from Burma (Myanmar), which only further increased the flow of opium from Southeast Asia.

Before World War II, the British government had considered a gradual suppression of opium smoking in Burma. At the time, they supported the prohibitionists' views, popular in the League of Nations measures and that of the United States, as we saw in chapter 4. Britain's colonial government in Burma preferred only a slow elimination of opium and few economic disruptions, since opium sales continued to produce lucrative profits. However, the United States

---

8. McCoy, *The Politics of Heroin*, 33–34.

government pushed for the complete prohibition of opium, which led to tensions between the British and American governments.[9]

The Burmese colonial government also came under pressure from Burmese nationalists, who wanted to end the practice of opium smoking. The nationalists blamed the continued use of opium on British colonialism. In 1939, U Kun, a representative in the Burmese legislature, pushed for a resolution calling for a total prohibition of opium and alcohol.[10] The British-controlled Burmese government did not support the resolution, arguing that farmers would suffer from the loss of revenue and that prohibition infringed on personal freedom. The British government later gave in to pressure from nationalists because of losses to the Japanese. In November 1943, the United Kingdom announced the total prohibition of opium smoking in all British territories, including Burma. However, the British government's announcement had little impact in Burma since by that point, the country was occupied by Japan. Japan announced a three-year abolition plan of its own, but never fully implemented its plan because of war disruptions.

Both during and after the war, tensions developed between government leaders' military and political objectives and their desire to eliminate the drug trade. During the war, opium proved enormously valuable to Allied forces fighting the Japanese in Burma. The British military paid the Kachin people (a confederation of ethnic groups) opium from India to fight the Japanese.[11] Opium use, widespread among the Kachin and the Burmans, allowed the British to gain control over the region. Thus, the necessities of war trumped pressure to end opium use. A similar situation occurred in French Indochina, as the end of the war created a foundation for an opium-based economy in Southeast Asia. This expanding opium market during World War II worried American anti-drug activists, but the need to win the war always took precedence.

United States officials also used opium in Burma to acquire support to fight the Japanese. Members of the Office of Strategic Services (OSS), an American wartime intelligence agency, funded and conducted guerrilla operations in Burma using opium as a primary tool.[12] Colonel William R. Peers and Dean Brelis of the OSS detachment 101 later explained the importance of opium in their operations in Burma:

> Our decision to use opium was based on the fact that it would give our troops a certain amount of freedom, of buying power; we did not question

9. Ashley Wright, *Opium and Empire in Southeast Asia: Regulating Consumption in British Burma* (New York: Palgrave Macmillan, 2014), 140–41.

10. Wright, *Opium and Empire in Southeast Asia,* 144.

11. Wright, *Opium and Empire in Southeast Asia*, 147.

12. William Walker, *Opium and Foreign Policy: The Anglo-American Search for Order in Asia* (Chapel Hill: University of North Carolina Press, 1991), 163.

it as just or unjust . . . Simply stated, paper currency and even silver were often useless, as there was nothing to buy with money; opium however, was the form of payment which everybody used. Not to use it as barter would spell an end to our operations . . . If opium could be useful in achieving victory, the pattern was clear. We would use opium.[13]

From these words, we can see that opium continued to be a major commodity that had a central role in the local economies. Even though some US officials wanted to end opium production in Southeast Asia, the priority for those participating was to win the conflict. To Peers and Brelis, opium became a means to an end.

Meanwhile, in South America, World War II impacted the production of cocaine. Anti-cocaine activists in Peru and the United States attempted to limit the production of cocaine, which failed as coca production, intertwined with the local culture, was continued for medicinal products. During World War II the United States government strengthened its position against cocaine production, as it attempted to spread what US officials believed to be superior American values. The war forced South American governments into a closer working relationship with the United States and severed connections between South American businesses and Germany and Japan.[14] As a result, the Peruvian government mimicked the US drug policy. The war also destroyed cocaine production in Germany and Japan, the largest producers of cocaine products. The United States came out of the war as the only country with significant medical cocaine production capacity. At the same time, the US government maintained a goal to lower use of the drug around the world.

The changes in the market for coca leaves allowed for the anti-cocaine movement in Peru to gain ground. This movement received support from US institutions such as the Rockefeller Foundation, which produced studies demonstrating the need to end cocaine use.[15] This connection allowed for more US influence at all levels of Peruvian society, which increased US authorities' leverage over Peru's government. With the limitation of legal markets for cocaine, some Peruvian producers turned to the illegal market. There existed a strong demand among consumers in the United States and globally for cocaine, but due to the domination of anti-cocaine proponents in the United States, the legal market could not meet this demand. The illegal market also moved into Colombia. After World War II,

---

13. William Peers and Dean Brelis, *Behind the Burma Road* (London: Robert Hale Ltd., 1964), 261.

14. Paul Gootenberg, *Andean Cocaine: The Making of a Global Drug* (Chapel Hill: University of North Carolina Press, 2008), 226.

15. Gootenberg, *Andean Cocaine*, 229–30.

smuggling of cocaine by small criminal syndicates started to increase but continued at a small scale until changes during the Cold War increased production.

Postwar Drug Trade: Cold War Politics

After World War II, relationships between the capitalist United States and the communist Soviet Union represented a new form of imperialism and a driving force behind global integration—that is, globalization. US efforts to contain the spread of communism in Asia involved forging alliances with ethnic groups and warlords who inhabited the areas of the Golden Triangle (an expanse covering Laos, Thailand, and Burma). These partnerships provided the Americans accessibility and protection along the southeast border of China. US and French officials supplied some of these warlords and their armies with ammunition, arms, and air transport for the production and sale of opium. This resulted in a major increase in the availability and illegal flow of heroin into the United States and Europe.[16] At this point we need to remember that while this volume is not focusing on addiction, that is another factor. Drugs moved quickly into the commercial mainstream after alcohol prohibition failed, and producers continued to find ways to promote their product after World War II.[17]

Starting in the late 1940s, the region known as the Golden Crescent (Afghanistan, Iran, and Pakistan) continued as the largest producer of opium for the global market due to the French Connection. At first, Southeast Asia only produced small amounts of opium because of the anti-opium reformers' suppression efforts. Since Southeast Asian farmers produced little opium, local merchants and users turned to the global opium market. Demand in Southeast Asia grew, so opium flowed into the area from Iranian traders linked to French and Thai opium cartels, as well as Chinese smugglers from Yunnan Province.[18] This extensive trade highlights the global nature of the illegal opium market.

After Japan had been defeated in China, Chiang Kai-shek and his nationalist government plunged back into a civil war with the Chinese Communist Party led by Mao Tse-tung. The United States government supported Chiang's forces, but by early 1949 the communist forces started winning. To support his fight with the communists, Chiang's forces funded their war by trading opium across Southeast Asia. Meanwhile, Mao's communist forces started an opium eradication campaign. This created a problem for the US government. On the one hand, the Americans needed to support the nationalist forces in China to fight

---

16. McCoy, *The Politics of Heroin*, 90.

17. Courtwright, *The Age of Addiction*, 127.

18. McCoy, *The Politics of Heroin*, 87.

communism. On the other hand, those forces provided opium to the regional opium market, which the US government was attempting to dismantle. Since the fight against communism took precedence, members of some US governmental agencies aided or ignored the drug smugglers, while blaming the drug trade on communist forces.

Opium production became a facet of Cold War politics in China and Southeast Asia. Harry J. Anslinger, director of the Federal Bureau of Narcotics, believed that noncommunist control of China and Southeast Asia protected American values, and that the spread of communism and the spread of drug use were intertwined. Anslinger contended that the communists spread the illegal drug trade, and only by supporting Chiang's nationalists could the opium trade be totally suppressed.[19] Anslinger's argument was not accurate, however, as Mao's communist forces had attempted to eradicate the opium trade. The communists argued that the damage from opium and heroin use was a result of the capitalist and imperial oppression of the West. Interestingly, Mao promoted state-monopoly cigarettes to replace opium smoking.[20] Anslinger was aware that the Chiang government used opium to fund his fight against the Chinese communists, but he hoped that if the United States provided more support to Chiang, the Chinese nationalist leader would abandon the opium trade.

After the Chinese communists defeated Chiang's nationalist forces in 1949, Mao's new government worked to suppress opium production. Five months after the communists created the People's Republic of China, Zhou Enlai, the first premier, signed an order titled "Concerning the Strict Elimination of Opium Poison," launching an anti-opium campaign.[21] The Chinese communists were serious about stopping the opium trade and considered it a perfect example of the evils of capitalism and imperialism. In practice, however, stopping the trade proved difficult. The production and trade in opium provided economic resources for several regions of China, and while the communist government attempted to replace the opium market with other products, it failed at first. The isolation of the People's Republic of China, combined with the outbreak of the Korean War, cut the country off from the rest of the world, which aided the government's efforts.[22]

By the early 1950s, narcotics officials in the United States started to abandon the idea of eradicating the opium trade in Southeast Asia. Anslinger still used the

---

19. Douglas Kinder and William Walker III, "Stable Force in a Storm: Harry J. Anslinger and the United States Narcotic Foreign Policy, 1930–1962," *Journal of American History* 72, no. 4 (1968): 912.

20. Courtwright, *Age of Addiction*, 76.

21. Kathryn Meyer and Terry Parssinen, *Webs of Smoke: Smugglers, Warlords, Spies and the History of the International Drug Trade* (New York: Rowman & Littlefield, 1998), 268.

22. Meyer, *Web of Smoke*, 274.

Chinese communists as a scapegoat, claiming that they produced and sold opium on the international market, even though the opposite was true.[23] Publicly, the United States took an active role at the 1953 United Nations Opium Conference, calling for an end to the illegal global trade even as certain government officials continued to support opium warlords as a tool to fight communism. While Anslinger pushed for stronger sanctions, the desire to have allies against communism outweighed the push for protecting Americans from drugs.[24] A similar problem arose for the French government, as they pushed for an end to the opium trade while using the drug to support their interests in French Indochina. As we will see, this concern about communism in Southeast Asia also played into US actions regarding drugs in Vietnam.

After the Chinese communist victory in 1949, the United States continued to support Chiang's government, which retreated to Formosa (Taiwan) and the surrounding islands. Opium production continued to be a part of this relationship. The outbreak of the First Indochina War (1946–1954) complicated the issue. In 1941 the communist Viet Minh, led by a Vietnamese nationalist named Ho Chi Minh, started to push for the liberation of Vietnam from French colonial rule. After the French colonial forces did not leave Vietnam in 1946, Ho and the Viet Minh started a war of liberation. Opium production played a role in this conflict. Vietnamese communist propaganda used the opium trade as an example of the oppression of French colonialism and capitalism. The wars in Vietnam were not just an example of the nationalist movement's drive to end Western colonialism, but also a conflict between the spread of the American and Soviet empires. This struggle between the Soviet Union and the United States in Vietnam changed the global drug trade by increasing the production of opium in Southeast Asia, as well as creating new trade routes.

For some members of US President Harry Truman's administration the fight against communism outweighed stopping the drug trade, and this fight would actually increase the illegal trade. While not the only reason, the support of various French and American military and intelligence personnel aided Southeast Asia in becoming self-sufficient in opium production by 1950.[25] Even though the communists defeated the Chinese Nationalist Army (the Kuomintang or KMT) in 1949, the nationalist government in Taiwan continued to oppose communist forces in Southeast Asia. In Burma and Thailand, the Central Intelligence Agency (CIA) aided the KMT along the Burma–Chinese border due to fear of a communist Chinese invasion. The KMT used weapons provided by the CIA to help increase opium production by the Burmese hill peoples by bartering

---

23. Walker, *Opium and Foreign Policy*, 189.

24. Kinder and Walker, "Stable Force in a Storm," 923.

25. McCoy, *Politics of Opium*, 91.

these weapons for raw opium. The Chinese nationalists shipped the opium to Thailand, where the Thai police transported the product to Bangkok. Criminal syndicates then shipped the opium to new markets in Malaysia, Indonesia, and Hong Kong. Meanwhile, French intelligence officers, desperate for funds to fight the Viet Minh, took over control of the opium production efforts. This new drug trade route highlights the intertwining of Cold War imperialism and the process of global economic integration.

By 1951, the members of the French Mixed Airborne Commando Group (Groupement de Commandos Mixtes Aèroportès, or GCMA) became involved in the opium trade in Vietnam. The opium traffic (known as Operation X) incorporated members of Corsican crime syndicates and corrupt French officials with the goal of fighting the communist Viet Minh.[26] The GCMA provided funding and equipment to the Hmong farmers who produced large amounts of opium (See Figure 5-1). The opium, stored in GCMA warehouses and transported on military aircraft, became a major part of the global market.[27]

FIGURE 5.1 The Hmong commander Vang Pao in Laos, 1961. The French and US intelligence forces depended heavily on the Hmong during the Indo-China Wars.
Source: Wellcome Collection. Attribution 4.0 International (CC BY 4.0)

26. McCoy, *Politics of Opium*, 92.

27. McCoy, *Politics of Opium*, 96–97.

After the French defeat in 1954, the US government stepped in to stop what they saw as the spread of communism. American intervention led to the Second Indochina or Vietnam War (1955–1975), fought in Vietnam, Laos, and Cambodia.[28] The war—officially fought between communist North Vietnam (Democratic Republic of Vietnam) and South Vietnam (Republic of Vietnam)—constituted a major expansion of the United States efforts to stop the spread of communism. The Soviet Union and China provided support to North Vietnam in the form of weapons and funds, while the United States deployed hundreds of thousands of US soldiers and used massive military force to dominate the region. Many US citizens and leaders claimed that the United States—the champion of freedom, democracy, and self-determination—needed to be in Vietnam.[29] Such ideals united a form of the Protestant civilizing mission with the new battle against global communism of the Cold War. Many Americans saw the Cold War as a struggle—or even a crusade—between themselves and a degenerate atheistic communism of the Soviet Union. The war and the military actions of the United States in Vietnam, Laos, and Cambodia will not be the focus of this discussion.[30] Instead, we will focus on the role the conflict had in increasing opium production in the region for the global market. The US government's concern about the increased drug use among American personnel also later aided in justifying the American global war on drugs.

When the First Indochina War ended in 1954, Vietnam became divided between the communist North Vietnam, under Ho Chi Minh, and South Vietnam, led by Ngô Dinh Diêm. The United States supported Diêm and the Soviet Union supported Ho. Central to the new Cold War tensions in the region was each side's distribution of the political, military, and economic influence. In the process, some US officials promoted an ideology of American superiority and a desire to save the people of the region from the evils of communism. The head CIA tactician for Vietnam, General Edward G. Lansdale, stated:

> I went far beyond the usual bounds given to a military man after I discovered just what the people on these battlegrounds needed to guard against and what to keep them strong . . . I took my American beliefs with me into the Asian struggles, as Tom Paine would have done.[31]

If we look closely at this statement, we can see that some American officials saw themselves and their actions in Vietnam in the same light as the heroes of

---

28. See Odd Westad, *The Global Cold War: Third World Interventions and the Making of Our Time* (Cambridge: Cambridge University Press, 2007).

29. Streets-Salter and Getz, *Empires and Colonies*, 487.

30. See George Herring, *America's Longest War: The United States and Vietnam, 1950–1975* (New York: McGraw-Hill, 2013).

31. Edward Lansdale, *In the Midst of Wars* (New York: Harper & Row, 1972), ix.

the American Revolution. Lansdale associates himself with Tom Paine, an author and political activist who inspired revolutionaries during the American Revolution. To Lansdale, the war in Vietnam consisted of a struggle to spread superior American values in opposition to communist ideology. To the communist North Vietnamese, the struggle consisted of their fight for independence and an end to Western capitalist colonialism.

Meanwhile, the Golden Triangle region continued to be a main supplier of opium, and intelligence officials continued supporting drug smuggling to keep various tribal groups in the region committed to opposing communism. Regional producers rendered processed opium into heroin. Two main trade routes fed the world market. The first and most important route ran from the Shan hills in northeastern Burma to Bangkok.[32] From there, the heroin moved into the international markets, with the largest being Hong Kong. The second route moved heroin from northern Laos to Saigon, in South Vietnam, and then to markets in Europe and the United States (See Map 5.1). By 1956, Saigon had become a major heroin shipping point in the international market. The growing chaos of war in the region allowed these trade routes to flourish.

In South Vietnam, Ngô Dinh Diêm's administration supported the illegal trade to finance its operations with Ngô Dinh Nhu, Diêm's brother and chief advisor, using money gained from opium for the repression of armed insurgency.[33] Nhu used Vietnamese intelligence agents and the Corsican organized crime ring as his contacts. From 1958 to 1960, Nhu relied on Corsican charter airlines for transport. The US government's desire to stop the spread of communism caused them to support corrupt and unreliable allies. By 1961 Nhu began relying on the US First Transport group, which flew missions for the CIA, to ship raw opium to Saigon for processing. In November 1963, South Vietnamese military officers overthrew and assassinated Diêm and Nhu with the knowledge and support some US officials. The United States government supported Nguyen Cao Ky as the new Premier of South Vietnam. Ky controlled the First Transport Group, and hence opium smuggling became a major part of the Vietnamese Air Force.

After 1961, US President John Kennedy started to increase the presence of American forces in Vietnam. Kennedy supported the Cold War foreign policy of his predecessors but believed that Diêm's forces needed to lead the way with American support. After Kennedy's assassination on November 22, 1963, President Lyndon B. Johnson moved to increase the number of American troops in Vietnam significantly. After that, the United States assumed even more of the

---

32. McCoy, *Politics of Heroin*, 152.

33. McCoy, *Politics of Heroin*, 153.

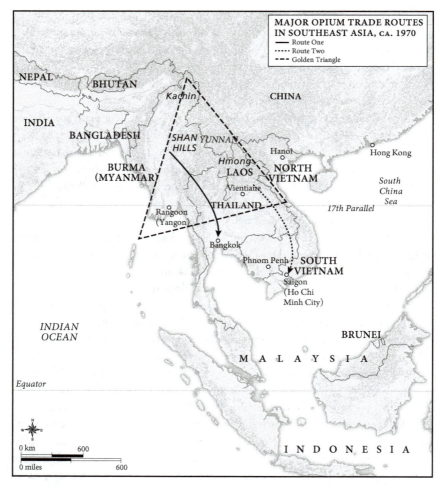

MAP 5.1 Major Opium Trade Routes in Southeast Asia, c. 1970

fighting. As larger numbers of American troops arrived in South Vietnam, drug use of all types increased. American forces came under immense wartime pressure and rising stress levels led to more drug use. As we will see, this increased American drug use had a major impact on the US perception of issues relating to drugs in Vietnam.

In Vietnam, American troops had easy access to legal and illegal drugs. The US military provided large amounts of alcohol to soldiers for recreational use. US personnel easily acquired beer and hard liquor either provided by the military or at local Vietnamese bars that catered to American soldiers. The military also regularly provided amphetamines to help soldiers stay awake on long-range reconnaissance missions or to lose weight. Soldiers also mixed Binoctal, a headache remedy, with alcohol to get high.[34]

The use and overuse of these legal drugs raises an important point. Many soldiers reported that the pills increased their irritability and led to more aggressive behavior.[35] The US Department of Defense (DOD) also reported that 88 percent of soldiers claimed to drink alcohol during their tour of duty, often in "prodigious amounts."[36] The military determined that 73 percent of enlisted men fit the definition of a "problem or binge drinker." Why did officials and the American people ignore this type of abuse? As we discovered, by the end of World War II, alcohol had become a major global commodity. After the failure of prohibition, activists focused instead on treating alcohol abuse. The expansion of the pharmaceutical industry as a global power was another factor in the spread of international markets of new types of synthetic drugs. These legal drugs were heavily promoted by manufacturers who were organized and politically connected, and encouraged their use.[37] Government officials around the world—led by the United States— saw recreational drugs such as opioids, cocaine, and marijuana as the major threat and needing to be banned (except for certain pharmaceutical and corporate uses).

In Vietnam, American troops used marijuana much earlier than heroin, with soldiers easily securing the drug in villages. We have not examined marijuana in this book, but we do need to briefly discuss its relation to heroin. In the 1930s anti-drug activists in the United States first added marijuana to the list of banned drugs they saw as dangerous. The US government banned marijuana and pushed for restrictions against it in other countries as well. During the Vietnam War military commanders initially tolerated marijuana, which many saw as less of a threat than alcohol (See Figure 5.2). Soldiers using marijuana created fewer problems than those using alcohol. One medical psychiatrist quoted in *U.S. News and World Report* in April 1970 remarked that "marijuana in Vietnam is cheap, easy to find and potent, the drug is everywhere. All a person has to do to get the drug in any village or town is say the word Khan Sa."[38]

This attitude started to change after January 1968, when John Steinbeck IV, a Vietnam soldier and son of the Nobel-prize winning author, wrote an article titled "The Importance of Being Stoned in Vietnam" for *Washingtonian*

---

34. Jeremy Kuzmarov, *The Myth of the Addicted Army: Vietnam and the Modern War on Drugs* (Amherst: University of Massachusetts Press, 2009), 17.

35. See Murray Polner, *No Victory Parades: The Return of Vietnam Veterans* (New York: Holt, 1971); Michael Herr, *Dispatches* (New York: Knopf, 1997).

36. Allen Fischer Jr., *Preliminary Findings from the 1972 DOD Survey of Drug Use*, Technical Report 72–8 (Alexandria: Human Resources Research Organization, 1972), 41.

37. Courtwright, *Age of Addiction*, 79.

38. *U.S. News and World Report*, April 6, 1970, p. 32.

FIGURE 5.2 Soldier smoking marijuana using the barrel of a shotgun nicknamed "Ralph." 1970.
Source: AP Photo/Jim Wells, File

magazine.[39] Steinbeck seems to have exaggerated the problem, but his article focused media and governmental attention on marijuana. Because of the efforts of anti-drug activists and government officials, the media and American citizens came to think of marijuana as a serious problem on a par with heroin. In response, the Army enforced existing laws, arresting over 1,000 GIs per week for marijuana possession. The American military, aided by South Vietnamese troops, searched out and destroyed marijuana-growing fields.

In response, many GIs shifted to heroin, which was odorless and harder to detect. As we already discussed, South Vietnamese officials, with the aid of French and US officials, had fully established the heroin trade throughout the region. American soldiers started using heroin because of the stress of a war that continued to expand with no clear end in sight. According to historian Jeremy Kuzmarov, there were multiple reasons for widespread drug use in Vietnam: it was "in part because we [in the United States] had the counterculture, in part because of the ready supply of the drugs, and in part because of the breakdown in morale in the Army, where a rebellion took root."[40]

---

39. Kuzmarov, *The Myth*, 23.

40. Kuzmarov, *The Myth*, 38.

Government officials and the media perceived the issue differently. Starting in 1966, Senator Thomas J. Dodd warned about drug use among US soldiers. He later argued that US soldiers committed atrocities because of their drug use.[41] After 1969, journalists published articles demonstrating how members of the media saw the problem. These stories pushed the idea that the military had been overwhelmed by addiction and that stoned soldiers hurt the war effort.[42] Recently other historians, such as Kuzmarov and Marilyn Young, have demonstrated that those government officials were wrong.[43]

What impact did increased media coverage have on society back in the United States? American citizens and government officials started to worry about addicted service members coming home and increasing the heroin market in the United States. Indeed, opium/heroin production and transport from the Golden Triangle increased, leading to more use within the United States by the civilian population. This fact did not stop the US government from focusing on returning American soldiers.

The United States government increased its efforts to stop drug use in South Vietnam via President Richard Nixon, who put pressure upon the South Vietnamese government. Nixon's actions indicate the influence of the American empire over other nations. Between 1969 and 1971, the US authorities provided narcotics training to thousands of South Vietnamese National Police officers.[44] Ironically, US officials provided anti-narcotics funding and training to the National Police at the same time some National Police officers shipped heroin to the international market. The US government also cracked down on soldiers in Vietnam and returning home from the war. Drug-addicted soldiers became a major concern of many US citizens and officials. In 1971, in response to this anxiety, the Nixon Administration implemented Operation Golden Flow, which mandated that all soldiers receive a urine test before boarding planes back to the United States.[45] If service members failed to pass the drug test, they stayed in South Vietnam for detoxification.

---

41. Kuzmarov, *The Myth*, 50–51.

42. Lee Israel, "Turn On, Tune In and Fire Away," *Washington Post*, February 9, 1969, p. 23 and Lee Israel, "A New GI for Pot," p. 24; Lee Israel, "Short-Timer GIs Deep Into Drugs," *Washington Post*, August 20, 1971, p. A18; Lee Israel. "Marijuana: The Other Enemy in Vietnam," *U.S. News & World Report*, January 26, 1970, p. 68.

43. See Marilyn Young, "Still Stuck in the Big Muddy," in *Cold War Triumphalism: The Misuse of History After the Fall of Communism*, ed. Ellen Schrecker (New York: The New Press, 2004), 262–273.

44. Jeremy Kuzmarov, "From Counter-Insurgency to Narco-Insurgency: Vietnam and the International War on Drugs," *Journal of Policy History* 20, no. 3 (2008): 349.

45. Kuzmarov, "From Counter-Insurgency to Narco-Insurgency," 353.

While the fear of addicted American soldiers fueled an American war on drugs, the spread of the war into Laos and Cambodia and the instability in Southeast Asia expanded opium production for the international market. Participants in this the international heroin market included Hmong and Vietnamese farmers; US, French, and South Vietnamese officials; Taiwanese Chinese nationalists; Chinese, Corsican, French, and American organized crime syndicates; and a customer base that spread from Asia to Europe to North America. The market had developed into a fully global endeavor. US combat operations in Vietnam ceased in March 1973, when the last US forces withdrew. The US fight to stop communism in Vietnam had failed. Its attempt to halt the drug trade in Southeast Asia failed as well. The thriving international heroin market, coupled with the anti-war protests, fear of communism, and the popular image of certain drugs in the United States, moved the US government to declare a global war on drugs in the early 1970s.

As we saw earlier, when World War II ended, cocaine smuggling by small criminal syndicates increased but remained small-scale until the pressures from the Cold War increased production, helping solidify the policy link between drugs and national security. The US government and the pharmaceutical industry emerged from World War II with more influence than ever before.[46] The Cold War accelerated the United States government's goal to sustain and expand its global position. The US government's global capitalist vision included the chemical and pharmaceutical industry, which supported America's consumer culture and the capability for the country to face global challenges.[47] Political and economic expansion in Latin America became central to this vision, especially as the Soviet Union—to further its influence—supported small communist groups throughout the region. Latin American countries provided a wealth of crops, including coca, that could be used for a variety of drug commodities. Before World War II, Merck, the international German pharmaceutical company, had close ties to the United States. In the late 1940s this position strengthened due to the US government's rebuilding of a postwar Germany. George Merck, president of the US subsidiary of Merck, became central to US drug policy and the expansion of pharmaceutical imports and exports. The coca industry became a major focus of this relationship.

The coca plant became a central part of the expansion of American imperial power. The desire to control the cocaine market not only focused on the pharmaceutical production of Merck in America, but the expansion of other legal coca products as well. The selling of American products globally not only expanded American capitalism, but promoted American political power and cultural value in the fight against communism. This can be seen in the global spread of Coca-Cola.

---

46. Reiss, *We Sell Drugs*, 72.

47. Reiss, *We Sell Drugs*, 71.

In South America, for instance, American companies such as Coca-Cola gained a monopoly over legal coca production. The company imported coca leaves to the United States, where they were de-cocainized for use in the drink. The increase in legal production and the domination of the production of coca by companies like Coca-Cola had a major impact on Peruvian coca farmers. The famers lost all control over the market and could only legally deal with select American companies. Some Peruvian coca farmers, facing poverty, had to turn to supplying the illegal market with cocaine to survive.[48] Later, many of these farmers were forced into partnerships with South American drug cartels.

Between 1947 and 1964, a new class of international cocaine traffickers appeared made up of a mix of Peruvians, Bolivians, Cubans, Chileans, Mexicans, Brazilians, and Argentines.[49] These traffickers from Latin America rose up because of the increased demand for cocaine in the United States and Europe and the increased production of coca for American companies. As examples of this, we will examine developments in Peru and Colombia.

In Peru in the 1950s, Andrés Avelino Soberón rose up as the main producer of cocaine paste for the local and international market.[50] Soberón, known as the "Johnny Coca-Seed" of South America, provided most of the cocaine for the nightclubs and restaurants in downtown Lima, Peru. He and his son Walter used farmers in Peru and Bolivia to grow coca, which they shipped to factories in Bolivia for production into cocaine. The Soberón family also sold cocaine to illegal traffickers in Brazil, Chile, Colombia, and Cuba. However, by 1960, pressure from the United States led to a severe crackdown by the Peruvian government on illicit cocaine production. As a result, Soberón lost his control over Peru's cocaine industry. After Fidel Castro took control of Cuba in 1959, cocaine also stopped being shipped through the island, as Castro's communist government pushed for heavy restrictions on the drug trade. In response to these developments, cocaine production shifted to Bolivia and Colombia though traffickers from all over Latin America were still involved. In the 1970s, cartels in Colombia became the major traffickers due various factors including changes to the global economy.

The Global War on Drugs

On December 21, 1970, US President Richard Nixon and rock n' roll star Elvis Presley had an impromptu meeting (See Figure 5.3). Nixon had grown concerned about the spike in the illegal global drug trade and drug use in the United

---

48. Reiss, *We Sell Drugs*, 132.

49. Gootenberg, *Andean Cocaine*, 245.

50. Gootenberg, *Andean Cocaine*, 259.

FIGURE 5.3 President Richard Nixon and Elvis Presley meet at the White House December 21, 1970. Later President Nixon coined the term "war on drugs."
Source: Ollie Atkins/National Archives and Records Administration/Wikipedia, https://en.wikipedia.org/wiki/File:Elvis-nixon.jpg

States. The counterculture of the 1960s, in which drug use featured prominently, alarmed political conservatives like Nixon. He hoped to shift young people's attitudes about drugs from a cool, trendy experience to one to avoid. As it turned out, it was Presley who contacted the president to ask if there was anything he could do to help the country. The singer, who collected law enforcement badges as a hobby, hoped in return to get a Federal Narcotics Bureau badge for his collection.

There is no transcript of the meeting, but a memo created later by an aide to the president offers a summary:

> The President mentioned that he thought Presley could reach young people, and that it was important for Presley to retain his credibility. Presley responded that be [*sic*] did his thing by "just singing." He said that he could not get to the kids if he made a speech on the stage, that he had to reach them in his own way. The President nodded in agreement.
>
> Presley indicated that he thought the Beatles had been a real force for anti-American spirit. He said that the Beatles came to this country, made their money, and then returned to England where they promoted an anti-American theme. The President nodded in agreement and expressed some surprise. The President then indicated that those who use drugs are also those in the vanguard of anti-American protest. Violence,

drug usage, dissent, protest all seems to merge in generally the same group of young people.

Presley indicated to the President in a very emotional manner that he was "on your side." Presley kept repeating that he wanted to be helpful, that he wanted to restore some respect for the flag which was being lost. He mentioned that he was just a poor boy from Tennessee who had gotten a lot from his country, which in some way he wanted to repay. He also mentioned that he is studying Communist brainwashing and the drug culture for over ten years. He mentioned that he knew a lot about this and was accepted by the hippies. He said he could go right into a group of young people or hippies and be accepted which he felt could be helpful to him in his drug drive. The President indicated again his concern that Presley retain his credibility.[51]

As we look closely at this memo, two key themes emerge. First, both Nixon and Presley agreed that illegal drugs are anti-American. The president argued that drug usage, public protest, and political dissent were all intertwined—weapons that challenged the status quo and threatened to upend American society. Second, illegal drug use in America, both Nixon and Presley concluded, was largely the result of foreign influence, most likely of the communist variety. By framing the domestic use of illegal drugs as a foreign threat, Nixon successfully connected his anti-communist foreign policy with his anti-leftist domestic politics. Hippies, supporters of the Black Power movement, and "Commies" were in league with one another, according to the president. Nixon coined the term "war on drugs" to highlight the new US government's global plan to combat illegal drugs.[52] But while much scholarship on the topic rightly focuses on the domestic impacts of this anti-drug policy—mass incarceration, overpolicing of communities of color, and the militarization of policing—this chapter focuses on the international dimensions of the war on drugs. Born in the United States as a domestic policy, the Cold War ensured that America's war on drugs was international in scope. Another aspect of the war on drugs is that while the trendy image of illegal drugs concerned President Nixon, this made up only a small part of drug use in the world. Illicit drug use was concentrated in the poorer segments of society who were the most vulnerable to the inducements of legal and illegal manufacturers and the ones looking for escape from their troubles.[53]

---

51. Memorandum for The President's File, "Meeting with Elvis Presley," December 21, 1970. The National Security Archive, George Washington University, https://nsarchive2.gwu.edu//nsa/elvis/test.htm.

52. "Nixon Calls War on Drugs," *Palm Beach Post*, June 18, 1971, 1.

53. David Courtwright, *Forces of Habit: Drugs and the Making of the Modern World* (Cambridge, MA: Harvard University Press, 001), 201.

In March 1972 the United Nations convened a conference, at the urging of the United States, to tighten controls over drug production. The United States government pushed for more control over opium and coca production by manufacturing countries. Producing countries as well as Soviet bloc states opposed this effort, because their governments considered it an infringement of national sovereignty and an expansion of American power.[54] American officials worked hard to gather international support for their effort to control production. Opponents succeeded in putting some limits into the new UN agreement, but for the most part the resolution followed American wishes.[55] The international drug control system concentrated on stopping the illegal supply of narcotics, but only succeeded in shifting production of heroin to Central and South America and increasing the production of cocaine.

As Soviet support for revolutionary groups in South America increased, so did CIA operations. Similar to the pattern in Asia, the Soviet Union and the United States competed for influence in Latin America, and drug trafficking followed the same pattern as that of Vietnam. This Cold War competition in Latin America played out in Honduras, Nicaragua, El Salvador, Panama, Cuba, Mexico, and Colombia.

Just as in Peru, under pressure from the United States, the Colombian government instituted restrictions on coca production. The unstable situation in Colombia led groups of various political ideologies to try to influence or overthrow the Colombian government. The unstable political situation only increased the power of two major drug organizations operating out of Colombia—the Medellín and Cali cartels. Both of these cartels started as small smuggling operations that realized the economic potential in exporting cocaine. In the late 1970s illegal cocaine production in Colombia became a major source of profit, due to poor economic conditions and the high international demand for the drug, with cocaine surpassing coffee as an export in 1982. The cartels allied themselves with businesspeople and politicians who raised private armies to fight off guerrillas who were trying to redistribute lands to local peasants, to kidnap them, or to extort money.

The Medellín cartel—led by Pablo Escobar, Gonzalo Rodriguez Gacha, and the three Ochoa Vazquez brothers, Jorge Luis, Juan David, and Fabio—developed from several smaller organizations. Exploiting the demand for cocaine in the United States and Europe, the cartel established connections across Latin America. George Jung and Carlos Lehder oversaw the trafficking routes through Panama and Mexico into Europe and the United States. The Cali cartel—led by Gilberto

---

54. William McAllister, *Drug Diplomacy in the Twentieth Century* (London: Routledge, 1999), 236.

55. McAllister, *Drug Diplomacy*, 236.

and Miguel Rodriguez Orejuela, José "Chepe" Santacruz Londona, and Helmer "Pacho" Herrera—initially cooperated with Medellín cartel, though in the 1980s the two became major rivals. The Cali cartel controlled poppy fields in Colombia and processing plants in Peru and Bolivia, with trade routes through Panama to Europe. During the 1980s, these two cartels controlled 90 percent of the cocaine market.

In Colombia, cocaine production became involved with political ideology and Cold War politics. Drug cartels, paramilitary militias, and various government officials and agencies formed alliances to further their interests. For instance, in 1982 members of the Medellín cartel, the Colombian military, Texas Petroleum (a US-based corporation), members of the Colombian legislature, and several wealthy landowners and businessmen formed a paramilitary organization, Death to Kidnappers (Muerte a Secuestradores, or MAS) to protect their economic interests.[56] Their main adversaries consisted of the military arm of the Colombian communist party—the Revolutionary Armed Forces of Colombia (Fuerzas Armadas Revolucionarias de Colombia, or FARC) and the National Liberation Army (Ejército de Liberación Nacional, or ELN).[57] FARC followed a Marxist-Leninist ideology, and had limited support from the Soviet Union, while the ELN received funding from Castro's communist government in Cuba. The United States and Great Britain considered both groups a major communist threat in Colombia.

To make the situation even more complicated, a right-wing paramilitary organization—United Self-Defenders of Colombia (Autodefensas Unidas de Colombia, or AUC)—fought both the FARC and the ELN to gain control of the Colombian government. The AUC worked closely with the Cali cartel and became heavily involved in cocaine production to fund its activities. CIA operatives supported the anti-communist AUC and later the Cali cartel in their conflict with the Medellín cartel, the FARC, and the ELN in Colombia.[58] While the ELN did not traffic in cocaine, the FARC turned to drug trafficking in the 1990s to compete with the AUC.

The war on drugs and the fight against communism only increased after the election of Ronald Reagan as president of the United States in 1980. Reagan increased funding to stop the drug trade and saw communist groups in Latin America as a major threat. The Medellín and Cali cartels increased their international ties in the 1980s, as they started to deal in heroin from Southeast Asia. During Reagan's administration some government officials worked closely

56. Jasmin Hristov, *Blood and Capital: The Paramilitarization of Colombia* (Athens: Ohio University Press, 2009), 65–68.

57. Hristov, *Blood and Capital,* 67.

58. Peter Dale Scott and Jonathan Marshall, *Cocaine Politics: Drugs, Armies, and the CIA in Central America* (Berkeley: University of California Press, 1992), 80–81.

with political groups and drug cartels across Latin America, while the US Drug Enforcement Agency worked to stop illegal production domestically.[59]

The Colombian drug cartels worked closely with criminal groups in Central America and Mexico. Colombian cocaine and Southeast Asian heroin passed through Panama with the aid of General Manuel Noriega, who controlled the military and government of the country. Noriega had close connections with the Colombian cartels and received support from the United States.[60] Cartel drugs moved through Panama to Nicaragua. There they were given to the Contras, a CIA-trained organization that attempted to overthrow the communist Sandinista government of Nicaragua. Here again Cold War conflicts became intertwined with the drug trade. President Reagan wanted to stop the Sandinistas, who were funded by Castro's Cuban government. The Reagan administration (through the CIA) provided support for the Contras, who were not only rebels but also a drug cartel, to overthrow the Nicaraguan government. The Contras received military and economic aid from the CIA, using this to become a major supplier of cocaine and "crack" cocaine to the American market.[61]

In the early 1990s, due to both internal and external pressures, the Colombian cartels broke apart and lost power as their leaders were killed or imprisoned. This created a power vacuum and a shift in global production. While cocaine production continued in Colombia, smaller organizations rose to control and diversify the market in both cocaine and heroin (See Map 5.2). While global economics changed after the end of the Cold War, the demand for drugs in the United States and European markets continued to expand.

In the late twentieth century opium production shifted from Vietnam back to the Golden Crescent, centering on Afghanistan. In April 1978, the pro-Soviet People's Democratic Party of Afghanistan (PDPA) seized power in Afghanistan. In response, Mujahedeen (Islamic resistance) forces started a civil war against the PDPA's government. In December 1979, the Soviet Union invaded Afghanistan in defense of the PDPA regime. The actions of the Soviet Union in Afghanistan paralleled those of the US government in Vietnam. During Russia's effort to defend the PDPA government, the Reagan administration aided the Mujahedeen forces, some of whom turned to opium production to fund their revolution.[62] The opium, converted to heroin, moved through Turkey to Europe and the United States. Once again, American officials aided in the global drug trade to combat the spread of Soviet influence. At first Soviet officials denounced the opium trade

---

59. Scott, *Cocaine Politics*, 44–45.

60. Scott, *Cocaine Politics*, 71–72.

61. For more on these connections see Scott, *Cocaine Politics*, and Gary Webb, *Dark Alliance: The CIA, the Contras and the Crack Explosion* (New York: Seven Stories Press, 1999).

62. Lukasz Kamieński, *Shooting Up: A History of Drugs in Warfare* (London: Hurst & Company, 2017), 301.

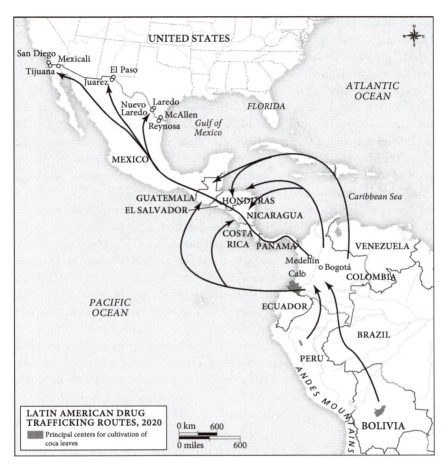

MAP 5.2 Latin American Drug Trafficking Routes, 2020

as a part of what they called "capitalist imperialism," but as the war in Afghanistan continued, they turned to trafficking in heroin for funding.[63] Similar to what had happened earlier in Southeast Asia, the conflict between the two imperial superpowers increased the opium trade in Afghanistan. Soviet forces withdrew from Afghanistan in 1989, but they continued to support the government until the Soviet Union's collapse in December 1991. After the collapse of the Soviet Union and the internal fighting among mujahedeen forces, the Taliban seized control of the country, which only set the stage for later conflicts in Afghanistan.

If we return to examine Latin America in the 1990s, several processes dominate the dynamics in Mexico. After the break-up of the major Colombian cartels, a new power structure emerged. Mexican cartels—the Sinaloa and Los Zetas

---

63. Kamieński, *Shooting Up*, 301–02.

cartels being the most powerful—filled the vacuum. At the same time, the United States started pushing for new free trade agreements. The North American Free Trade Agreement (NAFTA), enacted on January 1, 1994 and signed by Canada, Mexico, and the United States, created a trilateral trade bloc in North America. The agreement lowered trade barriers between the three countries with the goal of increasing wealth, jobs, and access to goods. The increased trade in North America, combined with the increase in global markets and spread of capitalism in the aftermath of the Soviet collapse, provided the perfect opportunity for the rise of the Mexican cartels. NAFTA tripled the volume in trade between Mexico and the United States.[64] This allowed the Mexican cartels to outcompete their global rivals for the lucrative US market in cocaine and heroin.

The struggle between communism and capitalism—primarily between the United States and the Soviet Union—to influence and dominate the world during the Cold War led to changes in globalization and the illegal drug trade. Illegal drugs continued to be central to the global market, as actions and choices made by political and military leaders, activists, and businessmen increased global economic integration. European imperialism had collapsed in the mid-twentieth century to be replaced by the end of the Cold War with a system of sovereign states committed to private ownership, market economies, and global commerce.[65] Transnational criminal organizations and coalitions of groups, who learned to move goods and people illegally over long distances, seized new opportunities. While the link between Cold War imperialism and an increased drug trade is not the only aspect of late twentieth-century globalization, it is an important facet of the complex relationship between capitalism, imperialism, and drugs.

FURTHER READING

Bagley, Bruce M., and Jonathan D. Rosen. *Drug Trafficking, Organized Crime, and Violence in the Americas Today*. Gainesville: University of Florida Press, 2015.

Felbab-Brown, Vanda. *Shooting Up: Counterinsurgency and the War on Drugs*. Washington, DC: Brookings Institution Press, 2010.

Kamieński, Lukasz. *Shooting Up: A History of Drugs in Warfare*. London: Hurst & Company, 2017.

Reiss, Suzanna. *We Sell Drugs: The Alchemy of US Empire*. Berkeley: University of California Press, 2014.

Steinberg, Michael K. "Generals, Guerrillas, Drugs, and Third World War-Making." *Geographical Review* 90, no. 2 (April 2000): 260–67.

---

64. Josiah Heyman and Howard Campbell, "Afterword: Crime On and Across the Borders," in *Smugglers, Brothels, and Twine*, ed. Elaine Carey and Andrew Marak (Tucson: University of Arizona Press, 2011), 180.

65. Courtwright, *Age of Addiction*, 159.

CONCLUSION

High Society

The face of "evil" is always the face of total need. A dope fiend is a man in total need of dope. Beyond a certain frequency *need* knows absolutely no limit or control. In the words of total need: "Wouldn't you?" Yes, you would. You would lie, cheat, inform on your friends, steal, do anything to satisfy total need. Because you would be in a state of total sickness, total possession, and not in a position to act in any other way. Dope fiends are sick people who cannot act other than they do. A rabid dog cannot choose but bite.

—WILLIAM S. BURROUGHS, *Naked Lunch*

William S. Burroughs, a prolific American author and heroin addict, wrote about the power of addiction and related drug use. Heavy drug use and addiction are a significant problem today, as we can see from the opioid epidemic sweeping across many countries. While addiction is a major factor in the success of the global drug trade, that is only part of the story. The argument of this volume is that trends and policies affecting the spread of globalization created and continues to support the global market in drugs. The drugs discussed in this volume are all addictive to one degree or another. However, as we have seen, while addiction separates drugs from other commodities on the global market, that alone does not explain the creation of a global drug trade. It was through the process of industrialization, commercialization, and imperialism that drugs spread across the globe.

The intent of this book is for you—the reader—to understand that the drug trade is not inevitable or unstoppable. This book has repeatedly emphasized the decisions behind the production and sale of drugs. As we have seen, political, ideological, and economic forces—each shaped by individual decisions—all shaped the way that global drug markets have functioned and changed over time. In today's world, it is easy to become overwhelmed by the problems of addiction or to stigmatize the inflicted as weak or criminal. Instead, the history of the global drug trade highlights the role of governments, businesses, and various groups and individuals in creating and shaping drug markets.

This book operates on the premise that knowledge of the past can provide an understanding of the process of globalization, as well as of the current drug market.

A common belief is that in order to stop the spread of illegal drugs, we must cure addiction and stop criminal activities. As we can see, there is more to the global market in illegal drugs. A clearer understanding of the history of globalization and why the trade in both legal and illegal drugs developed allows insight into a range of issues. This information also allows us to delve deeper into understanding the shaping of the modern world and our current society.

This volume looks at the creation of the global market in drugs from the fifteenth century to the collapse of the Soviet Union in the early 1990s. After the collapse of the Soviet Union, and with the aftermath of the decolonization movements, the global political landscape became more complex, as power structures shifted and new nations struggled for influence. The world altered again after September 11, 2001, and the attacks on the World Trade Center and Pentagon. Since 1990 China has become an economic powerhouse again, spreading their influence throughout the world. Geopolitical alliances and power structures have shifted, with international trade in drugs continuing on a global capitalist stage.

The markets for the drugs—legal and illegal—discussed in this volume are still thriving. In 2018, 9.5 million tons of coffee were sold, with Brazil and Vietnam leading production.[1] The global tobacco industry is making around a half-trillion dollars annually.[2] Alcohol in general has a mammoth global market, while rum specifically is produced not only in the Caribbean and South America, but Africa and Asia as well. Main consumer countries of rum are India, the United States, and the Philippines. As for opium and cocaine, the United Nations estimates that 1,410 metric tons of cocaine and 10,500 metric tons of opium were produced in 2018.[3]

If you use a web search engine to examine today's issues around addiction and the drug trade, the results from Wikipedia, government websites, international organizations, and major news outlets would lead you to believe that the illegal trade in cocaine and opium is the only issue. You would need to directly search for coffee or tobacco for those drugs to appear. Much of the discussion of the global drug trade centers on the addicts, or the drug cartels—leading us to believe that these depict the extent of the issue. As we have seen, the history of the global drug trade extends back to at least the sixteenth century and a wide variety of organizations, individuals, and government powers were involved.

A more in-depth historical investigation can lead us into a more nuanced understanding of the complicated and extensive global trade. You, the reader, can design research questions that would lead to a deeper historical investigation

---

1. International Coffee Organization, accessed July 1, 2019, http://www.ico.org/.

2. "Global Tobacco Market Report," *Cision PR Newswire*, March 15, 2018, https://www.prnewswire.com/news-releases/tobacco-products-global-market-report-2018-300614787.html.

3. United Nations Office on Drugs and Crime, *Analysis of Drug Markets: Opiates, Cocaine, Cannabis, Synthetic Drugs* (New York: United Nations, 2018), 7–8.

into various regions and societies. For example, in the introduction I discussed the impact of tobacco, opium, cocaine, coffee, and alcohol in various countries. Based on the model provided in this book, what would happen if you attempted to research these topics on your own? Possible questions that could aid you in this research include:

- What is the continuing role of legal opium and cocaine production globally, and how is it related to the illegal market in these drugs?
- How did Brazil become the major global producer of coffee in the world, and what was the impact on the local society and economy?
- How did multinational companies dominate the alcohol market in South Africa, and how does this link to past colonialism?
- How did the tobacco market in Turkey develop, and what was the role of the government?
- How did European imperialism, decolonization, and the actions of Cold War governments affect the development of these drug industries?

To address these research questions, a good place to start is by reading recent histories written by experts on the history of these regions. You could also look at the history of the political and economic imperialism of the region. After gaining a better understanding of the history of the area, you could then read scholarly articles and books that look at specific aspects of the history of any of these drugs. Scholarly treatments examining how the region links to the global market would also be useful.

When a news story on some facet of the global drug trade catches your attention, think about what the news account offers, and then inquire deeper into the topic. What questions are left unanswered? What are the major political, social, or economic issues, and how did they develop? Think about the historical background. Modern events were not created in a vacuum. What are the historical roots of any issue? A news article or internet search is only the beginning. Once you start researching the topic, new questions will occur to you. As you become better informed, you will be able to draw more accurate conclusions and make coherent arguments about how historical developments and societal and cultural factors influence policies and decisions, both in the past and today.

INDEX

Figures and maps are indicated by italic page numbers.

ABOUT THE COVER

The cover image is a photograph of smokers in a Beijing opium den in 1934. Opium became illegal in China during the Qing Dynasty, but after the dynasty ended in 1911 prohibition was only sporadically enforced. Even though opium smoking was illegal in 1934, people at all levels of Chinese society still consumed the drug. The photo was possibly staged due to the more formal clothing of the smokers, but it was quite common for opium smokers to lounge on a raised platform while they smoked. Photographer unknown.